Can We Wear Our Pearls and Still Be Feminists?

MEMOIRS OF A CAMPUS STRUGGLE

Joan D. Mandle

University of Missouri Press
Columbia and London

Library of Congress Cataloging-in-Publication Data

Mandle, Joan D.

    Can we wear our pearls and still be feminists? : memoirs of a campus struggle /
Joan D. Mandle.

      p. cm.

   ISBN 0-8262-1289-1 (alk. paper)

    1. Women's studies—New York (State)   2. Colgate University.   I. Title.

HQ1181.U5 M37   2000

305.42'07—dc21   00-029923

Text design: Stephanie Foley

Cover design: Vickie Kersey DuBois

Typesetter: BookComp, Inc.

Printer and binder: Thomson-Shore, Inc.

Typefaces: ITC Giovanni

For J

Contents

Preface

There were many difficult decisions associated with writing this book. But among the most important was how to handle the names of individuals who were part of the experience I was chronicling. After considerable thought, I decided to use pseudonyms for everyone about whom I wrote. I did this to protect the identity of the people with whom I interacted since I had not revealed to them that I was taking extensive notes on our interactions. In addition, in almost all cases, except that of women's studies itself, the departments of faculty members, the specific positions of members of the administration, and the majors of undergraduates have been disguised. On the other hand, it seemed foolish to attempt to hide the fact that I was writing about Colgate University. Since I was not using a pseudonym myself, it would be easy enough for anyone to ascertain that I had directed women's studies there.

Though my experience represents a case study and I only rarely generalize beyond it, in the most profound sense this story is about more than Colgate. It is about how a passionate commitment to feminism and social change is compatible with an inclusive and open intellectual engagement of ideas and views on women and gender.

Many individuals have contributed to this book. They have talked with me, helped me reflect on my experiences, and read and commented on the manuscript, giving me courage when I feared no one could understand both my hopes for and anguish about women's studies. They of course bear no responsibility for the views expressed in this book, but I thank them from the bottom of my heart for their love and support: Mike Burke, Pat Burke, Barbara Epstein, Lou Ferleger, Elizabeth Fox-Genovese, Adonal Foyle, Bonnie Hallam, Carol Joffe, Kelley Katzner, Jen Leigh, Laura Leith, Ami Lynch, Paul Lyons, Jay Mandle, Jon Mandle, Daphne Patai, and Karen Schupack.

*Can We Wear Our Pearls
and Still Be Feminists?*

Introduction

The idea for this book emerged from a conversation I had with a feminist scholar who twenty years earlier had founded a successful women's studies program at a major midwestern university. I spent several hours listening to what she referred to as her "war stories," tales of controversies and internal politics that had finally driven her out of the program she had created. "Life is great now!" she told me. "I am really happy to be back in the history department, teaching women's history and doing feminist research without all the aggravation of being part of a formal women's studies program." What struck me was how similar the problems she recounted were to those I had experienced since taking over as director of the women's studies department at a small liberal arts college.

Though my friend did not hesitate to express her deep criticisms, even reservations, about women's studies to me, she became tense and upset when I casually mentioned that I thought she should be writing about what had happened to her. Women's studies, I thought, could benefit from her years of accumulated experience. "Absolutely not!" was her dismayed reply. "We shouldn't be saying anything in print that might be interpreted as hurting other women or damaging women's studies. If we ever went public with these stories, they'd only give ammunition to feminism's enemies." I argued with her at some length, maintaining that telling the truth could strengthen the vitality of women's studies programs. Self-criticism was the only way to resolve the very problems we had been discussing. But she remained adamant and became alarmed when I jokingly said I might someday write up my

1

experiences. "It wouldn't do any good even if you tried," she warned. "No one will understand what you are really trying to say. They'll call you an antifeminist. It's impossible to be both critical and supportive at the same time. You'll be attacked by those who think you are too harsh and also by those who think you are too forgiving—it's no use."

It was soon afterward that I started taking notes on my experiences at Colgate. Five years later I began to write this book. In 1998, while it was under way, I had a déjà vu experience. As I sat chatting with a group of a dozen program administrators at the annual convention of the National Women's Studies Association (NWSA) the remarks of my friend, the historian, were repeated almost verbatim. A high-ranking NWSA officer laughingly began to joke about what she called "our stories from the trenches in women's studies." Another director joined in, "Wouldn't it be something if we could actually write down the problems and the fights and the debates we have gone through over the years in women's studies? It would be long; that I know!" "That's for sure," chimed in a third administrator, "but we'd have to be certain no one else ever saw it. We could never publish it. Women's studies has enough problems already and the Right would only use it against us. We shouldn't provide them with ammunition." "Well then," replied the NWSA officer, "I guess we'll have to write them up for ourselves and circulate them just for fun." The discussion soon turned to other issues, but I could not stop thinking what a shame it was that the only time I ever heard women's studies faculty admit to problems was in private, as part of personal conversations or off-the-cuff joking.

I, too, understand the pull of loyalty to an enterprise in which one believes and for which one has worked hard. The shortcomings of feminism and women's studies programs that I explore in this book are extremely painful to me. In fact, that is precisely why I feel so strongly about the need to air them fully. They need to be discussed, not only by critics of women's studies, but more importantly by its teachers, scholars, and students. Loyalty is misplaced and harmful if it hardens into an inability to be self-critical. To blindly support the status quo in women's studies programs, steadfastly denying the existence of significant problems and failings, is ultimately a far greater threat than any critic could ever be.

CHAPTER 1

Beginning

Before becoming director of women's studies at Colgate, I had never participated in a formal women's studies program. Indeed, I was somewhat skeptical of the effectiveness of such programs in a university setting. My academic home during the previous twenty years had been in sociology departments. As a graduate student in the late 1960s, before the emergence of women's studies as a discipline, I focused my research on the women's movement in the United States. Both my master's thesis and doctoral dissertation applied sociological theory to an understanding of feminism. Much of my research since then has built on that initial work. Teaching sociology over the years also permitted me to explore feminist questions, this time with students. Over the years some of my courses were concerned exclusively with women. In 1971, for example, Temple University's sociology department asked me to develop and teach a course devoted to the study of women and the women's movement. It was one of the first such courses in the country. In other sociology courses I have taught, the study of gender has also figured prominently. Emphasizing women and gender in the field of sociology became easier after 1972 with the establishment of Sociologists for Women in Society (SWS), an organization that promoted feminist scholarship and teaching within the discipline. With sociology increasingly encouraging the study of women, I saw no need to become part of an organized women's studies program.

But it was not simply my comfort working as a feminist academic within sociology that kept me from participating in women's studies. I had other concerns as well. I worried that immersion within women's studies might demand a narrowing of my intellectual perspective to an almost exclusive focus on women. Sociology had allowed me to pursue my interest in gender, while at the same time examining large social questions such as social movements, discrimination, and social justice. I was worried that women's studies would prove to be a less intellectually stimulating and fruitful way of thinking about gender than the comparative analysis that sociology encouraged.

I also had anxiety about teaching in women's studies. I did not want to limit my interaction with undergraduates to only the relatively small group of women students who were attracted to women's studies. Most of them were already aware of and committed to feminism. But my most exciting teaching invariably occurred when I introduced concepts of gender and feminism to students who had not been previously exposed to such ideas and who would likely never have signed up for a women's studies course. By folding gender considerations into sociological discussions of social change, social organization, poverty, the family, or education, I could effectively teach both female and male undergraduates about feminist issues. In this way, I was able to acquaint otherwise indifferent or even hostile students with feminist scholarship without threatening them. I was content to teach about women and gender in sociology courses and had little motivation to become part of a women's studies program.

One other issue bothered me. I knew that women's studies programs were sometimes associated with the identity politics that had come to dominate political life at many universities. I objected to the tendency to think that women were the only group worthy of study or that only women could understand or write about women. I feared the potential insularity of a field that many defined primarily by the gender of its scholars and students. I did not know if I would be able to hold back the pressure toward an inward-turning program, focused primarily on guarding its own gender-defined turf.

But there were positive aspects, too. I had come to respect the role that women's studies programs filled on many campuses. These programs were the primary source of pressure on traditional disciplines to integrate feminist insights into their courses. They supplied the impetus for the growth of specific courses on women offered in traditional fields, and they provided a home where feminist scholarship could be nurtured. Even today, this process is far from complete; the full integration of feminist contributions to traditional fields has remained only partial. Some disciplines have resisted including the study of women as an important part of their subject matter. Furthermore, even among those fields that encouraged feminist scholarship, courses dealing with gender were often the most recent additions to the curriculum and therefore the most vulnerable when departments were forced to limit their offerings. I knew that active women's studies programs still had important contributions to make. They could continue to ensure scholarly attention to women, as well as provide a place where students could concentrate on the study of women and gender.

These were the issues with which I struggled when I learned in November of 1990 that Colgate would be hiring a new director for its women's studies program. I had to admit to myself that the job was attractive. I had taught sociology at Colgate since the previous September on a leave of absence from my permanent position at Penn State. I liked Colgate—especially its strong liberal arts tradition and its emphasis on excellence in teaching. I also enjoyed the close interaction with students and the academic rigor of the place. Most importantly, I was impressed with the potential for an exciting women's studies program there. Though the college was relatively small, with twenty-seven hundred students, and had only been coed since 1975, it seemed significant that the women's studies program offered more than a dozen courses each semester. Furthermore, women's studies had about ten majors each year and a group of more than thirty faculty members committed to the program.

Nevertheless I had nagging concerns. Talking to students and faculty, I realized that some of my worries about insularity in women's studies seemed to apply to Colgate. It was clear to me that the program had made little effort to reach beyond those already committed to it. It had not communicated effectively with most of the students on campus. The result was that though there were many women's studies courses offered, the discussion of feminist issues on campus was confined to a narrow segment of the university.

Despite these concerns, the promise of women's studies at the school ultimately made the challenge of directing the program irresistible. I decided to apply for the position. When several months later I was offered the job, I accepted. By then I had spent a great deal of time thinking about what I would want in women's studies, and I had a clear idea of where I hoped to take Colgate's program. It would be self-consciously and publicly open, intellectually rigorous, self-critical, and creative. In this way, it could resist becoming the captive of identity politics. I wanted women's studies to forge strong connections with traditional disciplines and be welcoming to everyone on the campus. My goal was for the program, both in the classroom and beyond, to become attractive to students of all levels of knowledge and commitment to feminism. In women's studies they would find tolerance for their points of view and the chance to participate in stimulating discussions about important issues. The vision that led me to become part of women's studies was of a program both eager and able to provide every interested student and faculty member with the opportunity to reflect upon and be challenged by issues of gender and social change.

There were two groups of students, loosely associated with women's studies, who presented obstacles to my achieving these ends. Each had contributed to the dominant image on campus of feminism as narrow and insular. If I were to succeed in creating the kind of program I wanted, I knew I would have to try to win them over. Doing that would also help overcome feminism's negative stereotype on campus.

In the past, neither the residents of Pitten House,[1] the only all-women's dormitory, nor the students running the Women's Resource Center (WRC) had been interested in reaching out to others or encouraging discussion of feminism. Pitten was established to bring together students with a shared interest in feminism. Like other "theme houses" on campus, its purpose was to serve and build cohesion among the students who lived there each year. Although several women's studies faculty served as "faculty friends" of Pitten, occasionally eating dinner and holding discussions with the students, Pitten was not organized to function as an educational setting for more than its own small group of residents. Though perhaps unintentional, the reality was that by offering feminists their own separate living space, the college

---

1. All proper names in this book are pseudonyms.

actually encouraged the isolation of Pitten residents, many of whom were already alienated from campus life. This isolation between self-identified feminists and the rest of the campus was precisely what I would need to overcome.

The same issue of self-isolation was present with WRC. Unlike Pitten House, this student-run feminist organization had been organized ostensibly to educate the campus. Funded by the dean of students in response to students' requests several years earlier, WRC collected and displayed resources and books relating to women. It was housed in a small dormitory room and possessed an impressive array of feminist books and magazines. WRC used its budget to purchase materials and to pay students to monitor the collection. The problem was that its resources were rarely used. In fact, few faculty or students knew of WRC's existence. Even fewer made the effort to locate the out-of-the way dorm room or try to figure out when the resource center was open. Only the small group of students who worked there during the semester regularly came to WRC. Each year these students purchased additions to the library with the funds that remained after their wages had been paid and, as they described it, "handed down" WRC to a group of their friends who would run it during the subsequent year.

WRC members made no attempt to publicize the existence of the center or to encourage others to make use of its resources. When I asked WRC students what they did during "work hours," they reported that they studied, chatted with friends, and recorded their personal thoughts in the collective journal that sat open by the door. One student, Suzanne, described her time this way: "There really wasn't much to do, but there was this great yellow couch in the back of the room, so when I wasn't studying I would curl up on it and catch up on my sleep." What became clear as I probed more deeply into the functioning of WRC was that a small group of students had managed to turn the resource center into their own comfortable hideaway. That this was the case was confirmed by Carol, a women's studies major who was not herself a "member" of the WRC group: "I would never walk in there. It was a little clique, and they made it clear that they didn't want any 'outsiders' like me coming in." If WRC affected the campus at all then, it was negatively. The message it communicated to those who were aware of its existence was that feminists were an exclusive group, uninterested in anyone but themselves.

I was disturbed that WRC students were able to draw work-study wages for working on women's issues with no oversight from the dean's office or from women's studies. What made matters worse was that there was a conspiracy of silence concerning WRC. The administration provided funds to students who claimed the mantle of feminism, but then said nothing when the students failed to perform. It made a show of its sensitivity to feminism by generously funding WRC, but it never bothered to find out whether WRC was providing a worthwhile service to the campus. The university's hypocrisy was almost matched by the students' irresponsibility. WRC had wasted funds that otherwise might have been used to educate the campus about feminism. WRC students refused to concede (perhaps even to themselves) that they had failed even to try to advance the discussion of women's issues on campus. Clearly, this organization would not support the outreach and educational role I envisioned for women's studies.

Soon after my appointment as director, I proposed to the administration that we replace WRC with a new entity, a center totally housed within women's studies. In my plan to reorient the program as a whole, this new center would be pivotal. It would be my vehicle for outreach. Existing outside the formal classroom, the center could create programs to introduce students to the issues that animate feminism. In this way women's studies would meet students where they were and be able to draw them into dialogue.

I felt that everything about the center had to be strategically planned. The center's new name had to trumpet its open and inclusive nature. Naming was important—I had learned this lesson from pioneer feminists before me. As early as 1965, the United States' first major political group to arise in the second wave of feminism had, after much soul-searching, decided to call themselves the National Organization *for*— rather than *of*—Women. Similarly, in 1972, I had been among those "founding mothers" who had fought to give the new feminist caucus of the American Sociological Association a name that would not exclude men. We chose the name, Sociologists *for* Women in Society, for that reason.

Thus, when it came to naming the new center, I rejected the obvious title, "women's center," because I feared it might communicate gender exclusivity, implying that it was a place only for women. Without a clear signal that the center was for everyone, not only would male faculty and students tend to steer clear of it, but so too would many women, reluctant to be part of an environment that excluded men. I wanted to select a name that would make it very clear that identity was not a bar to participation, that the center was a place where both women and men could discuss gender.

It was also important to me that the word *studies* be part of the center's name. This I hoped would indicate that the center was a location where serious intellectual exploration of feminist issues took place. Including *studies* would also differentiate the aim of Colgate's center from the therapeutic and support activities directed exclusively to women that characterized many university women's centers. The center's connection to the classroom would also be emphasized. I suggested that it be called the Center for Women's Studies. It would be an integral part of the overall women's studies program, dedicated, like it, to encouraging an open and inclusive dialogue.

The center's location was also critical. In the proposal, I stressed the importance of placing the center strategically. It needed a visible location: one that would be a constant reminder to students that the Center for Women's Studies not only existed, but was an integral part of the campus. What I wanted to avoid was what I expected the administration to offer: a room buried in a large administrative or academic building. There the center would be lost, unable to develop its own character. Instead I wanted students to think of the center as an important part of the university, but also as unique—unlike any other entity on campus. I asked to have the center located in its own freestanding building, or in a centrally located space with its own separate entrance, easily visible from the main part of the campus.

The proposal also emphasized the size of the center. I wanted a large place. If it was too confined—a room like WRC—it could not be configured to meet the many purposes I envisioned for it. I pulled out all the stops and presented a plan for my dream center. My request included a library area housing gender-related books and publications, as well as feminist magazines, brochures, and flyers. I asked for several offices, kitchen facilities, a small seminar room, and a large classroom. The classrooms, I explained, would be used by women's studies courses but also could be offered to other faculty, encouraging them to use the center's facilities. With a variety of classes and lectures scheduled there, students not involved with women's studies could become familiar with the center and its programming. Finally, as if all of this were not enough, I suggested that the offices and classrooms should open onto a large, central, attractive meeting space, visible from outside the building, equipped with comfortable chairs, tables, reading material, and free coffee and tea. With this plan, the center would be able to function as a classroom, an attractive meeting place, and a discussion and research center.

Creating and maintaining the new center was clearly going to be costly. I was asking for the allocation of quite a bit of university space and extensive remodeling. But in addition I proposed a new paid position: a full-time internship in women's studies. To do all of this, the overall women's studies budget would need to be increased significantly. I argued that an expanded budget was necessary in order to achieve the center's ambitious goals. I also maintained that women's studies suffered under special handicaps as an academic program both because of its relatively recent appearance on campuses, and because of the stigma with which it was associated. In 1990 there was still widespread skepticism about the validity of women's studies and resistance to the serious intellectual discussion of feminist issues. To overcome these prejudices, the center's project of outreach would require a special effort. Only with generous financial support could women's studies overcome those stigmas, break out of its confinement to a narrow area of student interest, and reach a significant proportion of the student body. But with that support, I assured the college's administration, the center would provide an engaged and experiential learning environment that could benefit the entire university.

I expected opposition within women's studies to the kind of center I wanted to create because it so sharply contrasted with the previous direction of the program. My predecessor, Pat Roth, had placed a high priority on creating what she referred to as "community" within women's studies. Indeed, she and many other faculty members had made the creation of community an explicit goal. They worked hard to create strong interpersonal ties within the program and were proud of the fact that this differentiated it from most other departments. Although professors in history, music, physics, and other disciplines occasionally referred to themselves as a community of scholars, the creation of the internal solidarity that defined *community* within women's studies was clearly not a priority for most academic departments. Throughout the university, of course, faculty strove to create departmental atmospheres collegial enough to enhance their teaching and research. But fulfilling the personal needs of faculty or students was not taken as an appropriate primary aim for a discipline itself.

In contrast, in her annual reports between 1985 and 1989, Professor Roth repeatedly cites the creation of community among women as a central objective of women's studies.[2] In 1987, for example, she wrote:

> Women need to locate themselves in the present on this campus by satisfying particular needs that can only be satisfied by this kind of community. This was to be done primarily through informal non-academic activities: We do not separate the intellectual and academic part of our responsibilities from the pressing larger needs of women students and faculty.

The program's emphasis on building a women's studies community led inevitably to questions of who should be considered part of the program. Though criteria for admission were never made explicit, the program often acted in ways that discouraged participation by men as well as women faculty not teaching in women's studies. Its internal focus also meant that students who were not part of the program were seen as beyond the pale.

The emphasis on community was reinforced by a team of external evaluators that visited the campus to review the program in 1988. Composed of three faculty active in women's studies on their own campuses, the team approved of the program's preoccupation with

---

2. All quotations from and references to annual reports are taken from the yearly reports that each director of women's studies is required to submit to the dean of the faculty concerning the program.

its own internal development and with community-building, "as long as women's studies is marginalized on the campus." The evaluation team expressed strong sympathy with the program's declared need to tend to its own internal needs. The allocation of time and energy within women's studies programs to community-building was seen as necessary for their survival in higher education where, it was argued, sexist attitudes and discrimination prevailed.[3]

But with respect to Colgate, the evaluators' view that it was the program's marginalization that required community-building was almost certainly wrong. Indeed, the opposite was more nearly the case: it was women's studies' emphasis on building solidarity within its own community that was probably the source of many of the program's difficulties. Much of the resentment directed to it was the result of its excessive focus on nonacademic issues and its differentiating itself from the rest of the campus.

In fact, when the Colgate program was first established in 1985, both the administration and many faculty had welcomed and supported it. The university initiated a national search for a director, which resulted in the hiring of a prestigious senior scholar to head the program. Additionally, it generously funded the program, creating a new faculty position for the head of the program and providing her with the resources to carry out its mandate effectively. Subsequently, the administration encouraged and supported the development of both a major and minor concentration in the field.

Like most women's studies programs, Colgate's depended on faculty in other departments to teach its cross-listed courses. This help was forthcoming. With very few exceptions, humanities, arts, and social science departments contributed actively to women's studies by "loaning" their faculty to teach those courses. In the years after its founding, the expansion of the program continued steadily. Its funding from the administration for lectures and speakers increased, its course offerings grew, and it participated in a major curriculum study sponsored by the

3. This view of the university is shared by many feminists. In 1997 a conference at the University of Akron was organized with the purpose of examining the position of women in higher education; the conference was called "Toxic Towers."

Ford Foundation. In short, there was evidence of considerable support for and a serious commitment to women's studies at Colgate from both the university and its faculty.

Nonetheless, seemingly from the beginning, many women's studies faculty, and especially its director, firmly held to the belief that the college was implacably hostile to the program, as well as to what they referred to as the "special needs" of women faculty. In initially describing the program to me, the director and several women's studies stalwarts emphasized its victimized status on campus and the importance of its nonacademic goals in compensating for and coping with that hostility.

Professor Roth's annual reports explicitly affirmed the importance of creating community through "informal mechanisms such as discussions, suppers, informal gatherings and Brown Bag lunches, the kind of formal and informal social events which permit people to mingle and talk." Because it so emphasized community, women's studies came increasingly to be viewed by many administrators and non–women's studies faculty as nonacademic. The program's disproportionate attention to women's special needs raised suspicions about its legitimacy and seriousness. To many, women's studies seemed to be more about group solidarity than solid scholarship and teaching. And indeed, there was a basis in fact for this indictment.

Not surprisingly, soon after the establishment of the program, its initial broad-based support within the university began to erode. The fact that women's studies saw itself as dissimilar to other academic disciplines created serious difficulties. By 1988, just three years after its inception, a number of faculty and administrators worried aloud to the evaluation team about the director's "extracurricular profile" and her persistent preoccupation with matters other than scholarship and teaching. Others expressed concern that women's studies was becoming "an advocacy program which is separatist and exclusive in nature and seeks to impart a unitary and ideological point of view."[4] Hostility and alienation were growing on both sides. Lines

---

4. All quotes are taken from the 1988 outside evaluation of Colgate's women's studies program.

of communication between women's studies faculty and the wider university deteriorated along with mutual trust and respect. The program increasingly turned inward, preoccupied with creating its own community.

One of the first decisions I made when I became director was to avoid discussing my planned changes in the program with women's studies faculty and students. I chose this path because I was sure that if I did otherwise I would fail to win approval for an inclusive and outward-looking center. After all, the individuals I would have been talking to were those who had shaped and were comfortable with the program I was attempting to transform. I would have had to be explicit about my criticisms of the previous program. There was little hope that in such discussions we could come to agreement. In fact, there was every likelihood that I would be consistently outvoted concerning the program's future. Under such circumstances, I would come under great pressure to back away from my plans for reorientation.

Discussions with the faculty concerning any proposed changes would especially be handicapped because the five or six women most closely associated with the previous program were all associate or full professors. In contrast, those most likely to be open to my views were junior faculty members, without the job security associated with tenure. Given the hierarchical power relations between tenured senior professors and junior faculty members, I could expect the senior women to prevail. In addition, I anticipated that the handful of students majoring in women's studies would side with continuity. They had been comfortable participants in a program some of whose important parts I was hoping to dismantle.

Instead of consultation, what I planned to do was work all summer to put my ideas into motion and simply hand the women's studies faculty and its students a fait accompli, in the form of a new center, at the beginning of the fall semester. My hope was that my political isolation would be brief. I counted on the center to generate the support that would allow my changes in women's studies to be successful. My belief was that many students and faculty who previously had felt unwelcome would be drawn to center events. These individuals would constitute my core of support. I even dared hope that the center's success in expanding interest and involvement in the program might, in time, win over some of those in women's studies who I knew would see me as a threat.

But in adopting a go-it-alone approach I also knew that I would be exposing myself to a second kind of criticism. Not only would the center be attacked, but so too would my exercise of power. Within universities and especially within women's studies programs, a rhetoric of consensus decision making and consultation is routinely employed. In acting on my own, I knew I was violating the norm of nonhierarchical decision making to which many feminists claim adherence.[5] To them, my behavior would look unfeminist. Thus, with respect to both the substance of the new program and the method I was using to implement change, I knew that battles lay ahead.

In fact, I would have preferred to avoid the charge of elitism that was certain to come. But I would not have been able to achieve my objectives if I had attempted to do so in any other way. And the reality is that, despite the rhetoric of equality and consensus decision making, most women's studies programs are actually characterized by both inequality and hierarchical organization. Like other parts of academe, women's studies is made up of groups who command widely differing levels of power and social status. All of this stands in contrast to the antihierarchical rhetoric of sisterhood.

In response, some in women's studies simply deny the presence of inequality. Others acknowledge it but blame the university for forcing "male" hierarchical behavior on everyone, including feminists. Very much less frequent are honest discussions about the need for structure and hierarchy in women's studies. One successful discussion of these issues, however, did occur at the women's studies program director's preconference sponsored by the NWSA in 1996. There, the normally

5. Early feminists' desire to avoid structure and hierarchy made it almost impossible for them to effectively organize for social change, contributing to the movement's inability to expand beyond a core of constantly changing small groups. As the historian Alice Echols argues, the ugly personal conflicts and constant turnover characterizing women's liberation led to the virtual disappearance of that branch of the movement only a few years after it had played a central role in inaugurating the second wave of feminism in the United States. See Alice Echols, *Daring to Be Bad: Radical Feminism in America, 1967–75* (Minneapolis: University of Minnesota Press, 1990).

hidden tension between ideology and reality became explicit at a workshop entitled "How to Be a Boss." The workshop topic sparked intense interest among the directors present, with discussion swinging wildly between two poles. Some stood adamantly against hierarchy. They agreed with the director who worried that the exercise of leadership and power would result in our "destroying community and deserting our feminist principles." Consistent with this view, several mentioned how uncomfortable they felt having to tell others—especially women secretaries and faculty—what to do. "We are all such good friends in our department—we socialize together and celebrate each others' birthdays. I don't know how to be a friend and also get people to do the important things the program needs done. We can't have both standards and community."

Other directors, like myself, were impatient with such talk. Our argument was that the successful construction of a nationally respected women's studies discipline required its directors to provide leadership and set high intellectual standards. To effectively implement our vision of women's studies we needed to make, take responsibility for, and stick to tough decisions. One workshop participant put it bluntly: "We have to grow up from the seventies' kind of feminism, and stop pretending everyone is equal when they're not. In women's studies we're too concerned about being nice, on not insisting that faculty and students do what they're supposed to do." No agreement emerged from this workshop. But in it had been laid out, more clearly than I had ever previously experienced, this important conflict at the heart of women's studies.

Though I knew it was risky, I sent my proposal to the provost without showing it to anyone. When he called me in for a meeting, I steeled myself, marshaling my arguments against the rejection I was sure was coming. I had asked for more than I had a right to expect. But his reaction was not nearly as negative as I had anticipated. Ironically, it was not the ambitious nature of my plans, but only the future of Pitten and WRC that gave him pause. He wondered about the need for a center, given the presence of two already established feminist groups on campus. This was the crux of the matter. I argued that the inability or unwillingness of either Pitten or WRC to reach out to involve the entire campus in a feminist dialogue made the center essential. It would not replicate an emphasis on creating a "safe space" for women or on meeting the personal and domestic needs of a small group of students. Rather it would take responsibility for expanding education on women's issues beyond the classroom to the college as a whole.

To my delight, the provost signed on not only to the center's creation, but to virtually my entire wish list. He approved the internship, and he went along with my suggestion to reinvent WRC as the Center for Women's Studies. Most important, the provost agreed with my insistence that the women's studies program have complete control over the activities of the center. WRC's budget was redirected to expanding the library for the new center. Last, he provided the center with a wonderful, large, first-floor space adjacent to a centrally located dormitory and with the funds to remodel it. My fantasy of a center with offices, library, classrooms, and lounge was about to become a reality. Located in a highly trafficked area of the campus, with huge floor-to-ceiling windows and a large sign over its own entrance, the center's physical form reflected the welcoming and open atmosphere I hoped to create there. There were to be no secrets, no cliques, no fearful groups hiding away in their own space. The new center would be visible to everyone and its prominence on campus would, I hoped, contribute to its becoming a magnet for students.

To inaugurate the Center for Women's Studies, I planned a grand opening to take place a month into the fall semester. I invited the entire campus. Jamaica Kincaid, the prominent Antiguan novelist, was our guest of honor. I saw this opening celebration as my first opportunity to reach everyone with the message that changes were being made in the women's studies program.

Even before the grand opening, however, programming at the Center for Women's Studies had already begun in earnest. We organized a weekly series of Brown Bag lunches where faculty led discussions about their research interests. Friday Night Free Flicks—films on issues relating to women and gender—were screened at the center. We sponsored several local activists who talked about their work on reproductive rights and legal aid for poor women. Mini-teach-ins on current political topics and forums in which students reported on their gender-related research were also scheduled.

At the beginning, attendance at center events was disappointing. We typically drew only a handful of students. Those who came tended to be the same people over and over again—students enrolled in women's studies courses who already were interested in issues of gender. We obviously were not yet reaching the wider constituency of students and faculty. Only their active involvement could make the center the inclusive intellectual forum on feminist issues that it was intended to be. The grand opening was our chance to attract more people to the center.

We inundated the campus with publicity about the celebration, inviting everyone to share our huge "inaugural cake." Kincaid was well known, and I had asked the Swinging 'Gates, a student all-women singing group, to perform. The women who were members of the 'Gates were very popular on campus. I thought their presence might attract others, who like themselves, would ordinarily avoid a women's studies event. The forty singers of the 'Gates were in many ways typical of precisely that part of the student body that consciously shunned women's studies programs, but to whom I hoped the center would now be able to relate. Furthermore, I had heard the 'Gates sing, and they were really good. Their performance would lend the grand opening a festive air. By showcasing these women's talents, I could send a message about the center's inclusive aspirations.

Since I was not at all sure that they would be willing to be associated with a women's studies event, I was pleased when the 'Gates enthusiastically accepted my invitation to perform. But my pleasure was not undiluted. I knew full well that their participation would be a source of contention. To many campus feminists, the 'Gates were anathema. Most 'Gates members participated actively in the school's Greek system and were part of the "in" crowd on campus. Women like the 'Gates, it was assumed, could not possibly be feminists. For many, it followed that they had no place in women's studies.

But even before the performance became an issue, an incident at the celebration foreshadowed just how difficult it was going to be to create an inclusive center. The opening was called for the late afternoon, and as people started arriving I breathed a sigh of relief. I saw it would be a good crowd. I settled myself in a corner by the door, joining four women's studies students who were engrossed in conversation about equity for women athletes at Colgate. After a few minutes, a male student, whom I did not know, hesitantly stepped through the doorway. Discussion in my group came to an abrupt halt as he walked in and said hello to one of the students, Samantha, whom he obviously knew. He stood awkwardly next to our small group, shifting from one foot to the other. No one spoke until finally, introducing himself as Pete, he asked what we had been talking about. After some delay, Samantha finally broke the tortured silence. She responded with a blatant lie: "We were talking about menstruation—something you'll never understand. It's a woman's thing you know." Pete blushed with embarrassment and the group reinforced his distress by staring stonily at him until he finally turned and fled the center. The students watched him go, and then without missing a beat continued their conversation about athletic equity.

I was appalled. When I asked what they thought they were doing, Samantha's reply was affirmed by the nodding heads of the others: "Well, now at least he knows how we feel when men make us feel awkward or stupid." What was amazing to me was that these students seemed to feel no remorse for consciously humiliating Pete. On the contrary, they sounded proud of their action. They had punished him for the sexism they had experienced from other men. To them, his being male legitimated their hurting him.

Their cruelty was mean-spirited, but something else was at stake as well. They had driven away a student who was a likely supporter of women's studies, one of the few males who had the courage to come to the center's opening. I let the students know in no uncertain terms that their humiliating Pete was not only infantile but harmful to women's studies. Attempting to gain psychological retribution against sexist men by attacking whatever man happened to be nearby was not only unkind but perverse. Instead of drawing Pete in as an ally, their actions seemed intended to turn him into an enemy.

The students defensively insisted that I was exaggerating the importance of the incident. "It was just a joke. What's the big deal? He's only one guy." They of course were right that Pete's participation in women's studies was not in itself critical to the program's success. It did not really matter if he himself ever returned to the center. But there was obviously a larger point at issue with which the students and I were in fundamental disagreement. They were not interested in the center's aim of encouraging everyone to discuss and think through issues of gender and feminism. "It's not our responsibility to educate everyone about feminism," another student, Penny, protested. "Especially not men—they just don't get it."

But in this case, it was the women students who did not get it. The center did have the responsibility to educate others; that was its purpose. Not only did Pete's interest, signaled by his presence at the center, deserve to be taken seriously, but I was convinced that only if he and other students like him—both women and men—were welcomed would women's studies be advanced.

At that moment, however, I had no time to think further about how to deal with this problem. People were arriving for the celebration in earnest. It was clear that it had attracted a large crowd, and would, as I had hoped, succeed in heightening the campus's awareness of the center. Jamaica Kincaid cut the ribbon, officially opening the center, and after several short speeches, I introduced the Swinging 'Gates. They performed three songs, and received a rousing ovation. I looked around, delighted that everyone seemed to be enjoying the entertainment, and relaxed, believing that my fears about inviting the 'Gates to perform had been unwarranted.

But as soon as the celebration had ended, I was barraged with complaints from a number of women's studies faculty members and students. They made abundantly clear their disapproval of my inclusion of the 'Gates in the program. They objected both to the lyrics of the songs they performed, and to how the 'Gates looked and dressed. Professor Ghirmay's anger was typical: "Couldn't they choose other songs? What they sang made women seem weak and dependent. They defined women totally by their relation to men. That's inappropriate at a women's studies event." It was true that the three songs the 'Gates had performed were about love and relationships, and that one was a ballad recounting the story of a woman whose lover had left her. But these themes were not unusual in the standard pop music genre that made up the group's repertoire. In fact, with the exception of the ballad, it was impossible to tell whether the love songs were about women or men, about strength or weakness, about loss or gain.

Other criticism focused on the concert attire of the 'Gates: sleeveless, scooped-neck black cocktail dresses with short skirts, pearls, nylons, and heels. Several women's studies students echoed the view of Needa, a senior major, who declared that women "who dress like that are being exploited by a male idea of beauty."[6] Needa was furious that the 'Gates had been included in the center's program. "They're not even feminists," she protested. "Being there, they ruined it for me. What they stand for undermines women's studies, and feminism, too." In short, for Professor Ghirmay, Needa, and others, the 'Gates symbolized—in their dress and in their songs—women who were too interested in pleasing men, too focused on relationships and love. Such women, they believed, had no place at the center.

But there was more at stake than simply my invitation of a singing group. Those who objected to including the Swinging 'Gates, like the women students who had earlier embarrassed Pete, were—whether they knew it or not—fundamentally challenging the direction in which I wanted to take women's studies. I firmly stood against the use of dress or music or any criterion other than intellectual interest as a test for participation in women's studies. Employing personal choice— in clothing, hairstyle, musical tastes, or other aspects of identity— as a means of disqualifying potential participants undermined the program's educational purpose.

I was particularly exasperated at the women's studies faculty who seemed to want to police their students' lifestyles. As teachers, I thought they should encourage the widest possible exploration of lifestyles and political views among their students. It is up to the students themselves to choose what they prefer. I wanted the center to be an environment that avoided such narrow-mindedness parading as feminist ideology. This intolerance had no place in the women's studies program I was trying to build.

In discussing the 'Gates with Professor Ghirmay, I insisted that the best tendencies within feminism support freedom for women to choose for themselves. As faculty, I told her, our personal approval or disapproval of the group's looks or song selection should have no

---

6. See Naomi Wolf, *The Beauty Myth: How Images of Beauty Are Used against Women* (New York: Doubleday, 1992).

bearing whatsoever on our eagerness to encourage them to participate in women's studies. Furthermore, I pointed out, neither Professor Ghirmay nor I knew anything at all about the attitude of any individual "'Gate" toward feminism. Though I refrained from saying so, it seemed to me preposterous that in a debate with a sophisticated academic I was forced to make an argument about the irrationality of assuming that what people look like, wear, or enjoy singing indicates their politics or ideas. But there it was.

In the end, there was a practical payoff to including the 'Gates. To the surprise, if not consternation, of many of those who had objected to their being part of the grand opening, a number of the 'Gates became actively involved in women's studies. More than a dozen of those in the original group enrolled in women's studies classes over the next few years, and three, including the leader of the group, actually became majors. Other 'Gates were often seen at center activities, and a few even became regulars. But most importantly, the inclusion of the 'Gates and my defense of that decision had made the center's ground rules crystal clear. Women's studies was for everyone.

The resentment felt by some women's studies faculty concerning my insistence on inclusiveness at the grand opening did not by any means end there. Conflict reappeared soon thereafter, this time concerning a reception for new faculty. The reception had become a tradition within women's studies prior to my arrival. It was a social event, I understood, at which women's studies faculty welcomed new colleagues to the college each fall. I decided to continue the tradition. But instead of just a small social occasion, I would use it as an opportunity to introduce the substance of the new women's studies program to as many faculty and administrators as possible. I sent invitations to the women's studies faculty, to every newly hired faculty member, to department chairs, and to key administrators upon whose goodwill the program's funding depended.

What no one had bothered to tell me was that, in earlier years, only new *women* faculty and administrators had been invited to the reception with the women's studies faculty. As soon as the invitations had been sent, I began hearing from disgruntled women's studies faculty members. They were concerned that this reception would be a departure from what was done in the past. Professor Young, for example, worried that an inclusive reception would "hurt women's studies. Our receptions" she explained, "were always really important for building community within women's studies. With all the other people you've invited, that won't happen." Others explicitly objected to the inclusion of men at the reception. Professor Jasson disapproved strongly: "You don't see men inviting us to their receptions. Why should we always be the accommodating ones and include them in ours?" When I asked her from which receptions women faculty had been excluded, Professor Jasson walked angrily away from me without responding.

In the aftermath of these exchanges, I was concerned that no one would come to the reception. Women's studies faculty, annoyed at the invitation list, might boycott it. Others, leery of attending a women's studies event, might also stay away. But on the day of the reception the crowd that showed up was reassuring. In addition to most of the women's studies faculty, a large number of new faculty—both female and male—came to the reception, many accompanied by their department chairs. Several members of the administration who knew about the redirection of the program also showed their support by attending. Among them were the president of the university, several deans, the director of public relations, and even the chief officer for campus safety. As the crowd grew, I recognized this as a great opportunity. After introducing each of the women's studies faculty who was present, I gave a brief speech. In it, I outlined the program's organization and the center's purposes, emphasizing women's studies' new inclusiveness and openness.

What was so significant about that first reception was that it afforded me a way to reach out explicitly to many who previously had felt unwelcome in women's studies. Professor Roth had done little to inform or attract existing faculty. But the reception allowed a cross section of the university to learn of women's studies' new orientation. It also turned out to be a good way to network. Several department chairs, with whom I had not yet had a chance to talk, invited me to speak with their faculty about teaching cross-listed courses. In addition, I set up appointments to meet with three newly hired faculty members, two in history and one in art, all of whom were eager to teach in the program. The good feeling engendered at the reception smoothed the way for my obtaining departmental cosponsorships for several lectures and a commitment from President Jeffries to fund a major women's studies project in the coming year. The reception's welcoming stance toward faculty and staff had helped to turn critics of the program into allies.

Grumbling about men in women's studies, however, continued even after the reception. Before my arrival at Colgate, only one man, an anthropologist, was teaching in the program. Despite his token inclusion, there is no doubt that an underlying antimale bias was present in women's studies. Indeed, the male professor himself felt it. He told me that though he enjoyed teaching women's studies courses, he had never attended any other program activities: "I really was made to feel uncomfortable. I didn't know if I was really welcome." The reality is that in the exclusive women's studies community that Professor Roth had built, he was not welcome.

In redirecting the program, encouraging the active participation of men was a critical issue. I felt strongly that discrimination was intolerable, all the more so in a program whose very existence was rooted in the effort to end gender bias. I wanted to make it clear that all faculty members were potential contributors to women's studies.

For many of Colgate's women's studies faculty however, the presence of men was considered fatal. Professor Mouton, a psychologist, insisted that my policy of including men in the program would bring to it "the very people who are most hostile to women's studies and who will undermine it." I was astonished. I could think of hardly anything more unlikely than a faculty member teaching in women's studies specifically for the purpose of attempting to destroy it. In arguing for exclusion, others maintained that even well-intentioned men would subvert women's studies, albeit inadvertently. As one faculty member told me, "There are too many men around the center. No one will think it is feminist." The mere presence of men, these critics claimed, would harm women's studies, since men inevitably dominate groups in which both women and they are present. In such situations, men exercise control by speaking more frequently and insisting that their points of view prevail. Women invariably defer to men, both fearing men's criticism and desiring to please them. The result is that women self-censor and are effectively silenced.

This was a caricature. The truth is that professional women's active participation at all levels of the academic world is strong evidence that they are neither deferential nor silenced. At least in universities, these women do not need to be separated from their male colleagues to be able to say what they think. Generalizations such as these were certainly inapplicable at Colgate. It was easy to find examples of articulate women providing strong leadership within Colgate's administration and among its faculty and students; women who seemed to have no difficulty whatsoever in expressing their points of view with men present. Women held many formal positions of power as well, through which they set policy for the institution. They were heads of departments, top-level administrators, and the majority of student leaders on campus. For women's studies faculty to assert that they or other academic women needed safe space from which men were excluded in order to exercise authority or influence the university was to ignore reality.

Some, however, not only feared including men in the program, but anyone—including other women—who they believed had a view of feminism or women's studies different from their own. At a women's studies faculty meeting soon after the reception, Professor Tomlin challenged the new direction of the program and the new faculty and students being attracted to it: "I feel we are losing something. I am just not sure whether this is really a feminist program any more. I don't know what all these new people really think." She obviously believed that for women's studies to be legitimately feminist, it had to be an ideologically homogeneous community. Conflicting views of feminism or of women's studies were seen as threatening rather than as a diversity to be welcomed. Faculty like Professor Tomlin thought that only they could be trusted to create a truly feminist women's studies program.

In contrast, I insisted that enforcing limits on participation violated what is fundamental to academic life—nurturing and protecting multiple points of view. This required that a single standard be applied to all faculty members—female and male—in determining who can be part of an academic women's studies program. The only standard should be whether those faculty members, in their research or teaching, address in a scholarly way issues of gender and women's role in society. That was sufficient for admittance to the kind of women's studies program that I was building.

The inclusive faculty reception was symbolic of my campaign to eliminate homogeneous community as an explicit goal in women's studies at Colgate. Instead of internal solidarity as an end in itself, I wanted the program to be open to multiple points of view. An academic program should not resemble a closed group of friends who think alike. Instead, participants in women's studies should be united by two explicit goals: the education of others, and the promotion of teaching and research about women and gender. To either, the sex of participants is of no relevance.

An even more serious expression of opposition to my reorientation of women's studies emerged within the center itself. Almost from the beginning there was dissension. I knew the plan for the center's absorption of WRC would not go unchallenged, and I expected trouble from at least some WRC students. The fact was that though WRC had done next to nothing to promote feminism on campus, the center's existence threatened to destroy its near-total control of the feminist agenda—limited as that was—among Colgate students.

To minimize this hostility, I tried to co-opt the former WRC students by offering them a stake in the new center. I did not want them as enemies and attempted to find a way that we could work together to make the center a success. I offered each of them a work-study job as a "student assistant" at the center at the same wages and hours they had received at WRC. Although I had not initially planned to pay students to work at the center, I felt obligated to compensate the former WRC workers. It did not seem right to deny them the income they had anticipated earning before the center had come on the scene. Writing to each of them before the beginning of the semester, I carefully described the new organizational structure and the anticipated role of the center. I asked for their participation and support in expanding feminist education at Colgate.

At the end of the summer when students returned to campus, I met with each WRC student individually, reiterating my hope that she would be part of the center. I did make clear, however, that things would be different. The new job of student assistant would involve outreach as well as old-fashioned hard work. All but one of the nine WRC students agreed to come on staff at the center.

Though they accepted my offer of employment, a number remained angry over their loss of WRC. They were resentful of supervision by me and by Penny, the new women's studies intern, and they frequently complained about the amount of work. I explained that if we really were to have an impact on campus, hard work and cooperation were demanded of all of us—the student assistants, the center volunteers, Penny, and me. From their very first day at the center, however, many of the former WRC students fought me for control of the center and its agenda. The battle raged for most of that first semester.

The student who was to have been the "coordinator" of WRC led the resistance. Sally struggled against my direction of the center at every turn. Only with reluctance did she accede to Penny's or my requests and instructions, and at times she flatly refused to do what was needed. The other former WRC students joined Sally in forming a distinct clique within the center, remaining aloof from and uncooperative with other student staff members. They did little to disguise their opinion that the center was, as Sally often stated, "not really radical at all." Sally unrelentingly pressed me for changes in both the center's mission and activities. Claiming to speak for the entire student staff, she initiated angry confrontations both at staff meetings and when we were alone.

To begin with, Sally objected to the organization of the center. I had conceived of it as an umbrella under whose auspices individual students would carry out projects. I asked each student assistant to develop a plan with Penny for an activity on which she wanted to work alone or with a small group of others. Although center projects all required my approval, I willingly gave it so long as they were consistent with the general goals of educating and drawing other students into a discussion of women, gender, or feminism. The idea was for the students to largely run their own projects, depending on the center for funds, resources, and mentoring. My hope was that they would enlist the assistance of friends and acquaintances in the student body, thereby widening the circle of undergraduates who would relate to the center.

Sally was simply infuriated by these arrangements. In particular she objected to the fact that decisions concerning projects were not made collectively. In her view the only way decisions could be "truly feminist was by having everyone decide together what each of us should be doing." She also wanted frequent staff meetings—every few days—so that "we can bond as a community, get to know each other better, talk about where we want the center to go, and about how we feel as feminists at Colgate."

I made it very clear that hers was not the approach we would adopt. The kinds of discussions she wanted were fine, I explained, but not during staff hours. Instead of long group sessions, I wanted the students to devote their limited time at the center to working on their projects. Monthly staff meetings provided ample opportunity for the students to update one another on their work and for all of us to exchange ideas. There was no lack of talk. Penny and I met continuously with groups and with individual student assistants to help them on their projects. Wide-ranging exploration of feminist issues was a fundamental part of these discussions. But rather than being confined to the already converted student assistants, the aim of the projects was to extend the dialogue to the entire student body. Far from attempting to discourage general debate about feminism, gender, or women, the work the students were doing would enhance and extend it.

None of this satisfied Sally. So long as I refused to allow the primary focus of the staff to be internal, she was in opposition. But on this issue I would not budge. The center's main purpose was not to build good personal relationships among the staff, nor to ensure their bonding through consciousness raising. Its energy instead needed to be directed outward: toward reaching and drawing in other students and faculty. It was my responsibility, not that of the students, to worry about the center's overall functioning and direction. The students' job was to use the six or seven hours a week they worked at the center to educate others through their projects.

Through all of this, Sally's mantra was that the center was not feminist enough. She repeated over and over again her strong objection to its "nonfeminist" hierarchy: "With all these rules, working at the center is exactly the same as working at a regular nonfeminist job on campus." This of course was nonsense. I tried to explain to Sally that the "feminism" of an organization was not measured by whether it had rules or structure, but by the nature of its goals and by the extent its work challenged and altered sexism. At the center, the rules, hard work, and organizational structure were important because only with them would we be able to accomplish our goal of raising the visibility of feminist issues on campus. Our challenge was a difficult one—to communicate with those who harbored superficial stereotypes, lacked information, and, in the case of most college students, had not yet really made up their minds about women's studies or feminism. But Sally was not interested in anyone who was not already a self-defined feminist. She had convinced herself that my approach was quixotic; to her, trying to educate such people about gender was a waste of time. She would conclude our frequent conversations with the same refrain: "Nothing will change. Colgate is a sexist institution, and we can't do a damn thing about it."

Sally wanted physical as well as organizational changes at the center. "It's too much like an office," she would often say. "We need to make the center more comfortable, to make it our own space." She wanted "feminist music playing" and "the old yellow sleeping couch put by the door." I denied her requests, pointing out that the center was a library and a workplace. With a sleeping couch and music playing, its identity would not be sufficiently distinguishable from other student hangouts. I wanted it to be obvious to everyone that the center had unique goals to accomplish. While the present furniture was informal and comfortable, there nonetheless was a serious atmosphere that I wanted to continue to nurture, not undermine.

The posters hanging on the center's walls were another sore point for Sally. She wanted to replace them with those that had hung in WRC. The latter, in contrast to the ones I had selected for the center, were exclusively devoted to celebrating the female body. What I had put up was a mix: some actually had come from WRC, but others exhibited an encyclopedic range of issues and positions within feminism. My objection to the single-minded concentration on the female body of the WRC collection was the narrow message it communicated. In contrast, the center's display made clear that there existed a diversity of feminist interests and concerns. That was, after all, what the center stood for.

In the end, it became clear that what Sally really wanted was a center that she, and those who already agreed with her, could control. She wanted to express her views without opposition and discussion, without having to tolerate or even hear opinions contrary to her own. But I was simply not going to allow the center and its student workers to create an insular enclave where only their own needs would be met, where others could take it or leave it.

In light of our disagreements, I was only mildly surprised when, several days before the Thanksgiving break, Sally stalked angrily into my office and declared: "I don't know if I can be a part of this anymore. As a feminist I need a place where I and other feminists can do anything we want: paper the walls with lesbian posters and yell 'Fuck men' at the top of our lungs if we want to, without worrying about who we are offending. Working here is forcing me to compromise my feminist principles." I maintained my calm. I tried once more to convince Sally of the importance of a wide-open center. I attempted to distinguish for her between what was appropriate for the center and what was appropriate in her personal life. In the latter, she could choose her friends and associate with whomever she pleased. At the center, however, she had a job to do, which demanded that she deal with all kinds of people and all kinds of ideas. I did not try to hide the contribution to the center I thought Sally could make. "You're bright and articulate and you say you care about women's studies and feminism," I told her. "Students will listen to you—if you would only take the time and make the effort to listen to them and take them seriously. Screaming 'Fuck men' may make you feel good. But it sure won't change any of the things about the world that you say you object to."

Ultimately, I knew that Sally's belief that "talk is useless" meant that she could not continue to work at the center. She did promise to think about what I had said. But just before she left for vacation she was back in my office, issuing yet another angry diatribe: "This is impossible. We should all have an equal say in picking the center's projects, not just you and Penny. It's like a dictatorship here." I responded by telling Sally that she was fired from the center staff.

Though I worried that my tough stance toward Sally might alienate other staff, I felt compelled to take the risk. Otherwise I would have to watch as my plans for the center were undermined. To my great relief, however, Sally's leaving did not have the disruptive effect I feared. Once she was no longer there, the other WRC students, for whom she had claimed to speak, became increasingly involved in center work. They seemed to lose their need to resist Penny's or my ideas. In fact, everyone at the center was relieved; Sally's departure resulted in a less tense and combative working environment. As time passed, the dozen student assistants got along better and grew increasingly able to work together. By the end of the fall semester, the center was functioning smoothly and beginning to elicit a positive response on campus.

Not from everyone, however. A persistent nucleus of opposition to the center festered among the residents of Pitten House, the all-women dormitory. I was disappointed but not surprised at this development. As a campus theme house, the residents of Pitten were expected to organize educational programming and discussions on their theme for themselves and other students. And in the years before the establishment of the Center for Women's Studies, Pitten had been the location where most lectures and discussions on women and feminism occurred at Colgate. Therefore, not unlike WRC, Pitten students perceived the center as a competitor and a threat to their viability.

But serious problems at Pitten long predated the creation of the center. The primary difficulty was getting enough students to live there. Though Pitten had beds for as many as thirty-five students, in most years fewer than a dozen students wanted to live in the feminist theme house. Because dorm accommodations on campus were tight, each year the university filled the remaining places with other students who were not necessarily interested in feminism. The feminist students thus found themselves in the awkward position of being a minority in their own house. Not surprisingly, they complained bitterly about the difficulty of sustaining a "theme house" under such conditions.

The tensions created by this situation became endemic, but that was not all. Pitten seemed constantly plagued by the personal problems of many of its residents. As a result, women's studies faculty frequently were called on to intervene. The 1990 Women's Studies Annual Report complained, for example, that too much faculty time and energy were being devoted to dealing with Pitten students' emotional and interpersonal problems. As my predecessor, Pat, told me, "It was one crisis after another over there." The concern with interpersonal problems sapped both faculty and student energy.

Related to and compounding these internal problems was an external one. Many Pitten residents were seriously alienated from the rest of the campus. And hostility went both ways. On the one hand, Pitten students flaunted the fact that they lived in a separate residence, apart from the majority of students whom they believed to be conservative and antifeminist. At the same time, the house and its residents were widely stigmatized and negatively stereotyped on campus. Students at Pitten were ridiculed for living in the "dyke house" and were often shunned. It is impossible to know which came first: Pitten students' separating themselves, or their being rejected. What was painfully clear, however, was that these tendencies were mutually reinforcing, resulting in increased antagonism both from and to Pitten residents.

Despite all of this, I thought that Pitten possessed the potential to contribute significantly to women's studies at Colgate. The house could serve as one of several locations for feminist thought and education. To the extent that its interests and programs differed from those at the center, that would only add to the overall richness and diversity of campus activities relevant to women's studies. By coordinating events and projects at Pitten with those of the rest of the program, I hoped to build a strong tripartite program of feminist education that included women's studies classes, the center, and a residential unit. From the beginning, however, I was concerned that the Pitten students might be too alienated to accept or successfully involve themselves in the center's outreach mission on campus.

Soon after my appointment as director of women's studies, I approached the students living at Pitten to seek their support. From our conversation, it was clear to me that any suggestions I would make were going to be rebuffed. Pitten residents saw the center and the reoriented program only as a rivals that threatened their interests. Despite this, I tried to assuage their concerns by affirming Pitten's autonomy. I suggested that, wherever possible, we should coordinate and work together. In response, Rene, clearly the leader of the Pitten students, took the position that they would only work with the center if they were guaranteed a dominant role in determining the content of its programming. I of course could not consent to that. I repeated that

Pitten could choose their own programming and the center would do the same. The Pitten students, however, held firmly to their anticenter position, and an increasingly serious breach emerged between us.

Over time, as the center succeeded in attracting increasing numbers of students to its events and activities, Pitten residents became increasingly outspoken in their hostility. They began to publicly denigrate and criticize the changes in women's studies, and they explicitly encouraged students to avoid the program. Delia, a Pitten resident majoring in women's studies, made it known to other majors that she "never would consent to be in a senior women's studies seminar taught by Joan Mandle. I'd rather give up my major than do that." The Pitten students themselves largely boycotted the center, only rarely attending lectures or activities held there. Coordinating events between Pitten and the center became impossible.

In the meantime, the mandated educational programming at Pitten House deteriorated. Only a weekly Friday afternoon "tea and conversation," was a regular occurrence. These were attended almost exclusively by house members and a few women's studies faculty, and attendance was sparse. Pitten residents, however, had a ready explanation for this failure: it was my fault. They blamed the existence of the center for the problems besetting the house and for the lack of student interest in it.

Though I was disturbed by their attacks and increasingly annoyed by their attempts to undermine the center's work, I did not want to sever relations with the Pitten students. They seemed bent on excluding themselves, but they were still Colgate students, and I believed they should be welcomed as part of the center's dialogue. Throughout the semester therefore, Penny and I encouraged them, both individually and as a group, to become more involved. Early on, at a Pitten dinner that Penny attended, she solicited ideas for center projects and explicitly offered the center's resources and support to Pitten residents. In addition, both Penny and I tried to attend the house's Friday afternoon discussions, and we frequently initiated conversations there about how we might resolve the tensions that existed between us. Penny even sent special invitations for all center events to residents of the house. Nothing seemed to help; their hostility only grew.

In the midst of all of this, Gerry, a student I had never met before, responded to a request, printed in the first women's studies newsletter, for new ideas for center projects. She walked into my office one day, saying she wanted to work on women's reproductive rights. According to Gerry, she and her friends had been talking about doing something, but since they had never been to the center, they did not know what was involved. "Where do we start?" she asked. This was exactly what I had hoped would result from the newsletter's challenge—a student bothered by an issue related to women's studies who would turn to the center for support in creating a project capable of raising that subject for discussion or activism on campus.

I quickly called Penny in, and the three of us brainstormed about how to get the campus talking about women's reproductive rights. Penny suggested bringing in a speaker from a national pro-choice organization, Gerry thought some kind of petition drive might get students involved, and I proposed an informational poster campaign, followed perhaps by performances by a student agitprop group. We wanted to involve a larger group in the final decision, however. So several days later Gerry, joined by three of her friends who had also volunteered to help, by two student assistants at the center, and by Penny, came up with a plan for a campuswide Students for Choice meeting. Gerry took the lead and did a great job. The meeting drew over two hundred students—for Colgate, an astonishing number on a political issue. I think even Gerry was surprised when, by the end of the evening, over one hundred students had signed up for committees to work on an array of fronts and to plan other events. Gerry was ecstatic and full of ideas for follow-up.

In the afterglow of this success, I could not have been more un-prepared when Gerry arrived at my office later that week convulsed in tears. She was quitting the project. When she was finally able to explain what happened, I could hardly believe what I was hearing. While walking across campus earlier that day, she had been stopped by two Pitten residents who, she reported, berated her mercilessly: "When did you get interested in reproductive rights? Pitten's already working on this issue; we've got it under control; you're just messing it up. You don't know anything about feminism anyway!" When Gerry tried to suggest that they work together, they cut her off: "We'll decide what has to be done. You just leave it alone."

Gerry was thoroughly cowed. Because she was only a sophomore and her attackers were seniors; because she was enrolled in her first women's studies class and felt inadequate about her knowledge of reproductive rights; and because she did not know where she stood on numerous "feminist" issues about which they seemed so sure, she collapsed in the face of their criticism. She was crushed by the personal nature of the attack on her, all the more so because it occurred at the hands of people she looked up to as feminist leaders at Colgate.

Appalled at the thought that someone so motivated and talented could be so easily convinced that she had nothing to offer, I spent hours with Gerry that afternoon. I explained that the Pitten residents simply were jealous and threatened by her success. I assured her that they had no plans to educate the campus about reproductive rights. They had not even bothered to come to the meeting Gerry had called. At first Gerry was inconsolable: "I know they don't think I'm a feminist. They are so much more advanced than I am."

As the afternoon wore on, I worked hard to control my impatience with her insecurity. In as many ways as I could, I tried to convince her that her concerns about not thinking or looking feminist enough were absurd in light of what she was actually doing to help women: "Gerry, you know as well as I do that it's impossible to measure how feminist someone is by looking at what she wears—skirts, pearls, and makeup, or boots and flannel shirts. No one, no matter her claim to feminist credentials, owns an issue. Neither you nor I nor anyone else has the exclusive right to decide who learns, programs about, or discusses feminism." I told her what was obvious—that if the Pitten students really cared about women's reproductive rights, they would welcome her efforts. I also described some of the ongoing problems that existed between women's studies and Pitten residents, explaining that she had simply become a lightning rod for their frustration. Unable to block changes in the program or control the center, they had unleashed their anger against someone they thought vulnerable.

By the end of our talk, Gerry had changed her mind and decided to finish what she had begun. "They still scare me, but I really care about this project," she explained. Gerry was able to stand up to the bullying, and I too had learned from this experience. I would never again underestimate the potential for turf-fighting among feminists. Gerry went on to see the project to completion, culminating her work by organizing a full busload of Colgate students to travel the eight hours to Washington to demonstrate for reproductive rights at a national march. Some time later Gerry mentioned that she had called the Pitten students and personally invited them to participate in the march. They never showed up.

Though Gerry's project was salvaged, the Pitten students' behavior continued to rankle. I thought that perhaps it simply could be explained away as an example of the posturing or callousness that often occurs among students on college campuses. But it seemed more pernicious than that. It was an attempt to silence and intimidate, and what was worse, it was done in the name of feminism. That the Pitten students were angry enough to try to destroy a successful project concerning an issue they presumably cared about indicated how serious the strain between the center and Pitten had become.

Predictably, relations with the Pitten students worsened. Shortly after the incident with Gerry, I received a late-night phone call from Professor Mouton, a member of the women's studies faculty, asking that Penny and I attend an emergency meeting at seven the next morning with Pitten students and several "faculty friends" of the house. When I asked her the nature of the crisis, she replied cryptically, "All I want to say now is that we need to discuss some issues." When I arrived at seven the next morning, I found half a dozen Pitten students and five faculty members who had long been advocates for the house already waiting. Without any preliminaries, they launched into a criticism of women's studies, of Penny, the center, and most of all of me for neglecting Pitten House and for refusing to engage in "radical feminist" projects. They demanded that I increase my support for Pitten and coordinate all the center's activities through the house.

The 7 A.M. starting time and the short notice of course had warned me that there was trouble brewing. I came prepared to defend myself and the program. After listening to their litany of complaints, I went on the offensive. I detailed what was actually going on at the center, as well as the numerous times Penny and I had attempted to include Pitten residents. I reiterated our standing offer to consider supporting projects suggested by Pitten students and pointed out that, despite our frequent requests, none had yet been forthcoming. As a conciliatory gesture, I went so far as to offer to hire a Pitten resident as a student assistant with primary responsibility for communication and coordination with the Pitten students.

My willingness to hire someone from Pitten seemed to reduce some of the anger I had felt when I first entered the room. Throughout the two-hour meeting, however, the Pitten students' theme that the center as insufficiently feminist, never let up. Afterward, Penny was distraught. "I can't believe them," she yelled as soon as we were out of earshot. "Why would they lie and say that we've ignored them? They made us out to be their enemy, but we're on *their* side. I've tried everything I know to get along with them and support them. But from the very beginning, whenever I went to Pitten, they made me and the other student assistants feel awful. They acted like they were the real feminists and we were jerks—like we didn't have a clue about feminism. When I'd talk about the center, they just ignored me. I really think they've declared war! This is only the beginning."

I agreed. The meeting had not really resolved our problems with the theme house and its advocates. And in fact their resentment of the center only increased. My hiring one of their own housemates as a liaison changed nothing; Pitten residents continued to boycott women's studies programming. Though I had managed to contain their ability to seriously damage the center, I was upset that I had failed to heal the angry divisions among Colgate feminists. A small but significant subgroup continued to flatly reject my effort to expand and reinvigorate feminist education on the campus. And ultimately, because they and their advocates among the faculty saw the center at best as a competitor and at worst as an enemy, women's studies was denied the ideas and creativity that they could have contributed to the program.

Over the next few years, Pitten's problems with recruiting students as residents worsened. I joined with other women's studies faculty again and again in requesting from the administration changes that we hoped might reinvigorate the theme house. And despite the evidence of declining student interest, many of those changes were actually put in place: moving the location to a smaller building with only thirteen beds; transforming it into a coeducational "gender-issues house"; and stepping up efforts at recruitment through the Office of Residential Life. Nothing worked. By 1996, the number of undergraduates indicating a preference for living at Pitten for the next academic year had fallen to the disastrously low level of four. Though the newly appointed dean of housing was strongly supportive of the idea of a women's residence, with dormitory space in short supply even she had to admit that the theme house was clearly no longer viable. At the end of the spring semester she informed me that she had no alternative but to transform Pitten from a gender/women's theme house into a regular dormitory.

I called a special women's studies faculty meeting to relay the news. I reported the dean's intentions and opened the floor for discussion. Several faculty, especially those who could recall the early days when Pitten had been the only feminist presence on campus, were, as I had anticipated, furious at the closing. To my surprise, however, their anger was directed not at me, but rather towards the student body and the administration. They raged at the dwindling numbers at Pitten: "Why won't students stand up for what they believe? Aren't there any real feminist students on this campus anymore? I can't believe they don't understand how important a women's residence is for them on a male-dominated campus like this one." The administration and especially the dean also came in for blame. The faculty who were most upset simply ignored not only the dean's many previous attempts to save Pitten, but also her explicit public support for women's studies and for a women's theme house. Professor Kastro saw disaster everywhere: "She's just trying to hurt women's studies. What will she go after next? Colgate is so conservative and sexist that it destroys even the opportunity for women students to live together. We're all vulnerable if we let them close Pitten."

I found the whole scene incredible. Here was a group of faculty prepared to fight for a women's residence, even when the students themselves had clearly demonstrated a lack of interest in it. Even more remarkable was the fact that in their discussion of Pitten's importance, not a single faculty member mentioned its educational role. Though this should have been the primary concern of the faculty and was in fact the stated reason for the university's support for theme houses like Pitten, its potential value as a source of intellectual growth for the student residents was ignored. Rather, Pitten's advocates simply continued to take the puzzling position that an enclave that served very few should nevertheless be preserved.

The rhetoric was heated, swinging wildly between hurt feelings and hostility. Professor Ellis elaborated on Professor Kastro's earlier contention that women's studies would never survive Pitten's demise. She claimed that closing Pitten would precipitate a crisis that would "destroy all campus education on feminist issues." I did not bother asking her to explain how the living arrangements of a handful of students could jeopardize the women's studies program, especially with class enrollments strong and the center attracting more students each day.

Throughout most of this discussion, the strongest support for Pitten had been limited to a handful of faculty. There was, however, an argument—centered on the issue of safety—that stirred support for Pitten among almost everyone present. In fact, before long, the entire conversation had shifted to the issue of campus safety for women students. The consensus was that Pitten's loss would place women students in danger. Her voice shaking with emotion, Professor Lasky queried, "Without an all-women's dorm, how can women feel safe at Colgate? Pitten is the only safe space for women on campus." Others voiced similar concerns.

The basis for this position was a shared alarm about instances of sexual assault and date rape on college campuses. Some faculty had come to believe that coed living arrangements were responsible for this violence. Their support for Pitten's all-women residency was rooted in this association. They argued that dormitories where women and men lived together were dangerous to women because the very presence of men risked sex-related crimes. They concluded that only an all-female dormitory, like Pitten, could protect women.

I disagreed, pointing out that their argument was inconsistent with what we know to be true of campus sexual assault. The fact is that sexual aggression against women by male students does not typically occur when they live in proximity in the same dormitory. Rather such assaults overwhelmingly occur at parties, often in fraternities, where students—both male and female—drink excessively. The creation of all-female dormitories therefore, I suggested to my colleagues, was irrelevant to this serious problem. To focus on coed dorms not only wrongly targeted all men as the problem, but also failed to come to terms with the real source of sexual violence. Further, it reinforced false stereotypes of men as sexual predators and of women as weak and vulnerable.

Ultimately it was conceded by most that the argument associating coed dorms with sexual assault went too far. However, then Pitten advocates fell back to a new position: that men are incapable of viewing women as anything but sexual objects. A number of faculty argued that male and female students in coed dorms can never develop the kind of relaxed and friendly relationships necessary for a successful community. Women in coed dorms are unable to feel comfortable or be themselves. As Professor Bloch, a faculty member passionately committed to all-female residences, stated in what I think was all seriousness: "We need an all-women's dorm so that the girls can walk around without combing their hair, in fluffy slippers and pajamas in the middle of the afternoon, just like we used to do at Vassar." In short, they believed that women need to be separated from men, if not for safety then at least in the name of community.

To me, most of this was pure fiction or at best a caricature of the differences between women and men. Rather than wanting to live separately because there are unbridgeable differences between them, almost all Colgate women and men choose to live in coeducational dorms. Indeed, most college women and men report counting members of the "other" sex among their closest friends. This simply would be impossible if the alleged planetary distance between the sexes were real, or if women students felt they needed to coif and dress themselves with care every time they talked to their close friends. Indeed, I maintained that the kind of interaction made possible by coed dorms represented a healthy development. It allowed members of each group to view others as the individuals they are, rather than as representatives of their sex.

At last we had arrived at bedrock: the issue came down to whether we as a faculty should be encouraging separatism in the name of community. I staked out my position right away. I strongly objected to the notion that community could exist only among similar people who find ways to exclude and separate themselves from others. Single-sex environments are not necessary for community, I argued. On the contrary, supportive and mutually enriching relationships are often constructed from the close ties and support that can and does emerge among diverse groups. Especially on a college campus where the broad education of young people is our most important goal, encouraging the idea of cultures—sexual or otherwise—as separate, mutually hostile, and irreconcilable should be anathema.

In terms of the actual problem of Pitten's closing, even Pitten's strongest advocates recognized that none of this abstract discussion of safety and community was really to the point. The fact was that not enough students wanted to live in the dorm. In the end, to try and remedy this, Professor Tosco suggested that the women's studies faculty urge our students to live there. She especially singled me out for this task. "What about women's studies majors and the students working in the center?" she asked. "Can't you get some of them to live at Pitten? After all, they say they are feminists."

I was floored. I recoiled at the notion that anyone would expect students involved in women's studies to have an obligation to live in a special dorm. I thought it was outrageous for faculty to pressure students concerning their living arrangements. To do so seemed to me to abuse the influence faculty have over their students. On the contrary, I had been at pains to make students feel welcome and comfortable with whatever level of involvement or commitment they chose to make to women's studies. There was never any pressure on students who attended our programs to volunteer or work at the center, nor for those involved in the center to major in women's studies. Students would, and I thought should, rebel if women's studies, unlike other majors, carried with it housing, work, or other extracurricular requirements.

I explained all this to my colleagues and told them further that just as feminism should not involve a single way of thinking, neither should it demand conformity to a particular lifestyle. The threat in all of this was that residence at Pitten House would be used as a test of feminist commitment. To this, I could not have been more opposed. I made clear to my colleagues that I thought if our women students no longer felt the need for a theme house like Pitten, we should neither condemn them nor demand that they live there. Instead, whatever our own preferences, we should demonstrate our commitment to tolerance and diversity by supporting their choices. If students did not want to live in Pitten, it should close.

In the end, despite the faculty's predictions of imminent disaster, Pitten shut its doors without serious consequences either for women's studies or for women students at the college. It was true that the few women who wanted to live in a single-sex dorm were unable to do so, but Pitten had long since ceased to play an important enough role in the college's life to be missed by many others. With WRC and Pitten gone, organized student opposition to the center and its policy of openness and inclusion had disappeared.

CHAPTER 2

The Interns

The center I envisioned would have to have an intern. It needed the kind of full-time commitment that I could not supply, given my other teaching and research responsibilities. Otherwise, the center would have to depend on student volunteers to oversee its day-to-day operation. I knew that a center staffed by students would have a number of problems and that it ultimately would not get the job done. Like other voluntary organizations on college campuses, it would suffer from turnover and erratic commitment. The burdens involved in running the center would be too great for students, whose primary responsibility had to be to their course work. Furthermore, with only students in charge, the center might become dominated by a specific student clique. After all, that was the fate of WRC. Finally, the content of programming in an exclusively student-led center concerned me. Few undergraduates possessed either the experience or the vision necessary to create programs that could stretch students beyond their personal concerns. I wanted the center to take the lead in exploring areas with which Colgate students were unfamiliar.

However, hiring a professional to run the center also seemed unsatisfactory. I did not want to replicate the experience of many university women's centers that had such an arrangement. Often these centers lacked a strong connection with the academic program and functioned independently of women's studies. I wanted Colgate's center and women's studies to be fully integrated. This would avoid the competition and sometimes explicit hostility that exist between women's studies programs and campus women's centers. Furthermore, full-time administrators at most university women's centers are not academics. More typically, they are trained in counseling, student affairs, or higher education administration. This kind of background would not prepare them for the direction in which I wanted to take women's studies at Colgate. The center would not be primarily providing psychological support and counseling, nor servicing the personal needs of women students.

What seemed best was to hire a full-time intern each year to work with me in supervising the functioning of the center. My plan was to train and work closely with the intern during the year. In this way I could monitor what was happening at the center and retain the ability to shape its direction. Through my daily involvement, the center would remain fully integrated into the academic women's studies program, with the intern providing the constant on-site supervision the center required.

In seeking an intern, I had in mind a unique combination of characteristics. I wanted to hire a recent college graduate, someone close enough in age, and sufficiently extroverted, to motivate the undergraduates with whom she would work. However, I did not want her to look to the students to be her personal friends; as a staff member, she had to exercise authority. She had to be her own person, able to keep her distance socially from the students at the center. This was made all the more difficult because of Colgate's geographic isolation. There would be few opportunities for an intern to meet people her own age who were not Colgate students. What all of this meant was that I needed to find someone who was unusually mature.

I made a conscious decision not to consider any Colgate graduates for the internship. All of them were much too involved in established friendship networks on campus. This decision was especially difficult because two of my best students, each of whom would have otherwise been perfect for the job, wanted to be the women's studies intern. They each lobbied aggressively for the position, pointing out that as recent graduates they would have the twin advantages of a deep knowledge of the college and of already established working relations with students. I hated to turn them away, but I knew that even the most mature and professionally oriented Colgate graduate would not be seen as neutral by the students when she had to make the complicated decisions she would be called on to make as intern. I had to hire someone without that baggage. I needed to find an intern with no ties to Colgate, self-sufficient, yet friendly and able to work well with others.

Although the intern obviously needed experience with women's studies and women's issues, I was wary of anyone whose interests were too concentrated in that area. Someone whose focus in college had been narrowly on feminism might be handicapped in reaching out to and working with the diversity of students—feminist and nonfeminist, female and male—that I wanted to bring into the center. The women's studies intern I had in mind had to be committed to feminism but also willing to be critical of feminist orthodoxy. My ideal intern was both intellectually sophisticated and flexible, with interests that included but did not end with feminism.

She had to be an organizer—someone who understood how to motivate student involvement and outreach, and who was able to find satisfaction in juggling the hundreds of details that successful center projects would require. When eighty high school girls came to Colgate to talk about women and work, it was the intern who would have to be sure there were enough name tags, chairs, and box lunches for everyone. Finally, I did not want to hire someone who was just filling time after college, not knowing where she was headed. The intern should have clear career goals within which her women's studies internship made sense.

Any intern obviously would have to be able to work well with me. I was all too aware of my own idiosyncrasies—a straightforward, not to say blunt, style, and a need to know literally everything that was happening at the center. I also knew I would not be able to control my tendency to constantly bombard her with ideas, pushing to have the center do even more. In order to avoid driving her to distraction, I needed to find an intern whose working style was compatible with my own. Furthermore, though I planned to give her considerable independence and freedom, she would have to share my goals. Only with a common understanding and strong bond between us could the overall vision for the center be effectively implemented. Ultimately, the intern's fit for the job would depend on her willingness to accept me as a mentor.

I often wondered if anyone with such an unusual combination of characteristics actually existed, not just in my imagination, but in the real world. If she did, I also wondered how I would ever find her. I decided to cast the widest possible net in soliciting applications for the internship. I sent announcements of the position to career planning offices and to women's studies programs at colleges and universities nationwide. I had no idea if I would receive a single application. The thirteen-thousand-dollar stipend I was able to offer for the year was embarrassingly low, and Hamilton's isolation was forbidding.

To my delight, applications literally poured in. During February and March, not a day passed that I failed to find waiting for me yet another stack of 8 1/2 × 11" envelopes containing applications. But a different problem soon emerged. As I leafed through applications, it dawned on me how difficult it was going to be to determine which of these graduating seniors had the characteristics I sought. Almost all of them seemed to be smart, dedicated, accomplished, and interesting. Furthermore, recommendations from their professors consistently warned of the fatal error I would commit if I failed to hire their "outstanding" student.

In an attempt to narrow the field, I decided to require a writing sample. I wanted to learn three things: first, how well a candidate could write; second, how logically she could think about a complex issue; and finally, whether she had the political sensibility I sought. I mulled over and rejected several possible topics for the essay, including one that asked applicants about their willingness to work with fraternities on feminist programming, one that asked for a general essay on their definition of feminism, and one that inquired about the goals they would establish for a center for women's studies. None of these seemed right. I feared that the latter two questions would fail to elicit answers concrete enough to provide the information I needed, while the suggestion that feminists ought to be working with fraternities might seem so outrageous that it would confuse applicants.

In the end I settled on the question, "Should a male professor be hired to teach a course entitled 'The History of Women in America'?" Disagreement among feminists over this issue was frequent enough that the applicants would not easily discern the answer I sought— that men had the right and should be encouraged to study and teach women's studies. This was my litmus test for the openness and inclusion concerning women's studies that I was looking for. In addition,

I hoped that in making the case for male participation, candidates would reveal other attitudes such as their views on identity politics, men, women's studies, and feminism generally.

The essay idea worked. Each year, when I had to hire a new intern, the two-page responses functioned like a Rorschach test. They allowed me to discern differences among candidates whose résumés seemed otherwise almost identical. A pattern emerged in the essays, permitting me to eliminate several groups of applicants from the pool. First, I removed all those whose essays were inadequately thought through, poorly written, or both. Such individuals would simply not be able to handle the job. I rejected a second group as well, whose responses completely ignored the topic I had assigned. Many in this group wrote about abstract feminist theory or about feminism generally, or offered their ideas on related issues. Though they were perhaps trying to appear creative or independent, their ignoring the topic I had assigned augured poorly, I thought, for their willingness to be pragmatic and to accept my instruction. A third set of applicants did address the issue of whether men should teach in women's studies programs, but they equivocated, refusing to come to a decision. I eliminated this group of essayists because by attempting to offer both a "yes" and a "no" to my question, they seemed unsure of themselves or unwilling to say what they thought. I also discarded the few essays that relied on nothing but feminist rhetoric. These made my skin crawl, for they signaled just the kind of unthoughtful acceptance of feminist orthodoxy that I wanted to avoid.

Once the pool was narrowed in this way, I examined the actual content of the remaining essays. The attitudes expressed there generally fell into two main categories, only one of which qualified the authors for serious consideration. The first group, the unacceptable essays, were those that stated unequivocally that men had no place in women's studies or in feminism. Some of these essays indicated intolerance not only of men, but also of women whose feminism was seen as inadequate. In one such essay, an applicant wrote: "Only women who are committed to feminism and have really understood the oppression of women everywhere and throughout history are truly capable of teaching women's studies courses. The rest of the university discriminates against feminists. Women's studies is their only home."

An intern with such views would clearly having difficulty living with the center's policy of inclusion.

But there was always a group of essays that captured precisely what I was looking for. These applicants offered inclusive definitions of feminism, made clear their interest in pragmatic projects, and expressed an eagerness to reach out to everyone, including men, who cared about justice for women. One such essay concluded:

> A department like women's studies that focuses on liberating our minds from societal barriers and limited academic disciplines itself can not be exclusive. We have everything to learn from each others' experiences. Women's studies courses can succeed in their goal of educating for the eradication of rigid gender roles only if they provide models of spheres in which gender roles are flexible. The fact of both male and female professors as teachers of women's studies classes challenges the gender role structure which dictates that women should only be concerned with women's issues. To evoke a famous slogan: biology is not destiny!

In the end, it was prospective interns' writing samples that enabled me to select a group of candidates whose general political stance was consistent with that of the center. Initially I worried that using the essays for this purpose was illegitimate. After all, I was eliminating applicants on the basis of their political beliefs. Doing so seemed wrong. But in thinking more about it, I concluded that the specific nature of the internship in women's studies necessitated some test of the applicant's openness to and tolerance of a broad spectrum of views and attitudes. I did not care—and never asked—about the candidate's position on any specific issues relating to feminism, such as abortion, sexual harassment law, or pornography. But a commitment to basic social justice and a deep tolerance for a diversity of views were essential.

The irony was that in order to create a center that was politically open, I had to find a way to exclude intern applicants who were themselves exclusionary—who adhered to such a narrow definition of feminism that they would not welcome and work with women and men with different points of view. I could not hire someone who shut off ideas because she did not agree with them. I knew that eliminating applicants on political grounds would look as if I were doing precisely what I would not tolerate at the center. But a test to ensure tolerance of all points of view was different. The intern would have an enormous influence on both the center and the students there. She had to reflect the same sensibility of political openness on which the center was based.

Each year when I received a new pool of applicants, their essays, combined with information on grades, organizational experience, and extracurricular activities, led me to fifteen or twenty finalists. After extensive phone interviews, I invited two or three of them to visit the campus to spend a day with me, the current intern, and Colgate students. While I took into consideration both the students' and intern's opinions of each candidate, it was I who had to make the final decision. The only problem was that each year the young women I brought to campus for interviews were so impressive that it was always difficult to choose among them.

I was initially attracted to the application submitted by Penny, the intern I hired the first year, because of the intriguing combination of groups of which she was a part. She was active in her college's women's center, but she also belonged to, of all things, a co-ed fraternity. After Penny's application made it to the finalist pool, I called to talk with her about her experiences. In response to my questioning, she explained that in fact combining women's studies and membership in a fraternity had caused her considerable grief. With members of each group viewing the other as an enemy, it was often difficult for her to be involved in both. But it soon became clear that, however difficult, Penny had responded to this mutual hostility as a committed organizer: she had set herself the task of reducing their enmity.

She recounted the many hours spent patiently explaining to members of each group that its stereotypes and assumptions about the other were false. "I tell my friends at the center that all fraternities don't degrade and exploit women—that my fraternity has lots of strong women in it who run the house along with the men. At the same time, I'm constantly fighting with members of my fraternity house who malign 'those crazy radicals' at the women's center. People get really fed up with me sometimes." But when Penny organized a discussion about feminism at the fraternity house and one about Greeks at the women's center, lots of her friends in both groups came. "I actually think I changed some peoples' minds," she admitted.

Penny's initiative in bringing together opposing groups of undergraduates sounded like exactly what I wanted the center to do. Someone with her commitment to crossing boundaries seemed perfect for the internship. Furthermore, Penny was a good student and had written a beautifully argued essay. Nonetheless, I hesitated to make her an offer, because other than volunteering at the women's center, she actually had little experience with feminism. A classics major, Penny had taken only three women's studies courses in college. Even after she told me that it was her women's studies courses about which she felt most passionately, I still had some doubts. Would she be in sufficient command of feminist issues and literature to be able to hold her own in the debates that were certain to rage at the center?

As it turned out, it was a conversation with one of Penny's professors, a women's studies colleague whom I knew well, that won me over. I had called her hoping to learn more about Penny's feminism. My friend, Professor Leach, divulged something about Penny that she had not even mentioned in her interview: Penny's role in a student-run women's studies class. A deep division had emerged among students in the class right from the start. The majority had originally planned the class as a kind of sounding board, where each week they could talk about their own personal lives and experiences. A smaller group of students, later accused by the majority of being conservative and less feminist, objected to this plan. They spent most of the semester fighting to change the course's direction. They criticized its lack of intellectual rigor, saying that the weekly discussions were repetitive and boring. Instead, they wanted a more traditional classroom format, with assigned readings, written essays, and discussions focused on substantive women's studies and feminist issues.

According to Professor Leach, Penny was the clear leader of the smaller group: "She was amazing. Most of the other students were older than she and had more visibility and status as feminists on campus. But she went right at them, ignoring them when they said she wasn't feminist enough and accusing them of wasting an opportunity to discuss really important feminist issues. She's not only smart and articulate—she's brave!" After hearing this story, I knew I should hire Penny. Professor Leach concurred, adding "I know what you want to do at the center, and Penny is just the person for you."

She was right. Penny did a terrific job during the difficult start-up year at the center. Her experiences as an undergraduate stood her in good stead. She never gave up, even when WRC and Pitten students refused to cooperate with her. Although she was hurt by their personal attacks, she persevered, continuing to do her job and drawing an ever larger group of undergraduates into the center. With Penny's skill at navigating among diverse groups, by the end of its first year the center was bustling with activity, and women's studies majors were working alongside and talking to students who had no previous experience with feminist issues.

During the year, Penny and I talked almost daily about education, organizing, and feminism. Much of this talk was related to center activities, but we rarely confined our discussions in that way. Penny was eager to read and explore feminist scholarship relating to the women's movement and to changes in women's lives. She had missed doing so in college, so we ended up having an informal seminar to which we frequently invited students who had stopped by the center. I greatly enjoyed these conversations, for they often concerned something I had spent most of my adult life thinking about—the interdependence of social change, feminism, and education. Furthermore, our discussions had a pragmatic application, as we related theories and our own ideas about change to what we were trying to accomplish at the center. We would discuss how difficult it was to change attitudes, and how best to create the kind of environment where everyone would be free to say what they really thought.

These talks were also important because at the beginning of the year, things were inevitably slow at the center. Penny was discouraged because she would plan programs hoping for a packed audience, but then attract only a handful of students. On several days early in the fall, she had sat in her office for an entire morning without a single student stopping by. But she tried hard to stay in perspective. We would talk often about how difficult it was to remember that we were just at the very beginning of trying to make the center an important part of campus life. "If we think only in the short run," I would tell her, "we'll never sustain the effort we need to get to everyone eventually. Social change gets measured in unbearably tiny increments."

We both wanted to experiment with as many different organizing and educational techniques as possible. It was clear that no one method would work for everyone. Dividing the campus into what we thought of as constituency groups—athletes, Greeks, first-years, science majors—we brainstormed about the programming that would appeal to each. Penny spent hours meeting with student leaders on campus to learn how we could work with them to reach more undergraduates. We felt sure that if we could entice people into the center just once, on almost any grounds, they would be more willing to come again—perhaps next time even to talk about feminism. So in addition to our programs, we offered free coffee and tea every day, and encouraged faculty and student groups to use the center's facilities for their own meetings.

Penny and I also frequently discussed how best to use the talents of the center's student assistants. We wanted each of them to be an "ambassador" to the rest of the student body, talking about the center and involving her own friends in its programs. Penny was quite successful in this. She worked well with the student assistants, encouraging and mentoring them as they developed and implemented their projects.

Penny's own project for the spring was an effort to incorporate both sororities and fraternities in the center's work. She planned a month-long campus educational project on women and AIDS to be carried out by student assistants, members of the Greek system, and other interested students. Penny poured herself into energizing the project. It included lectures and panel discussions on women and AIDS, a fundraising three-on-three coed basketball tournament, students going door-to-door in the dormitories with information, and an educational poster campaign supplemented by articles in the student newspaper. The project really put women's studies and the center on the map, ultimately touching hundreds of Colgate students, faculty, and staff, as well as people from the local community. It worked as well as it did not only because of Penny's skill and hard work, but because she had selected a topic, AIDS, about which many students already cared deeply. She had found a way to connect with their own interests and then to extend them to feminist issues such as women's poverty and sexuality, drug abuse among women, prostitution, and social policies affecting at-risk women. Perhaps most important, by including sororities and fraternities, Penny had demonstrated that the center could work effectively with everyone on campus; that its rhetoric of inclusiveness was real.

When Penny left in May to pursue a career as a high school English and women's studies teacher, she confided to me that she had only one regret: "I never got to my goal of reaching every single Colgate student at least once with something about feminism." But she had clearly learned something about how to measure social change because she added with a smile, "I sure got a lot of them, though, didn't I!"

Just before she left, it was Penny who ultimately convinced me to hire Courtney, my second intern. While helping to solicit and then cull through applications, Penny noticed that one of the finalists attended a university where she herself had close friends. Penny suggested that she talk with two of her friends. They might be able to provide additional information, especially since both of them were active in the campus feminist organization listed on Courtney's application. I asked Penny to wait until all three finalists had completed their on-campus visits, but when Courtney actually emerged as my tentative first choice, I encouraged Penny to call her friends.

Again, my method of selecting interns caused me a pang of conscience. Personal contacts and inside information seemed to replicate the approach to which I and other feminists had long objected— the use of informal old-boy networks to influence hiring. Objections to such networks reflected the fact that they often exclude women, preventing them from competing on an equal basis with men for jobs. But here I was, relying on an "old-girl" network to obtain information about an intern applicant. Nevertheless I overcame my qualms. The qualities I sought were so difficult to measure or even to recognize that I had to allow myself to grasp at any and all information I could obtain. In using these networks, moreover, no one was given an inside track. In fact, I was as eager to learn why I should not hire an applicant as I was to be convinced that she was the perfect choice.

Penny reported that the campus women's organization in which her friends and Courtney were involved was very similar to the center. "My friends have goals like mine," she said. "We all learned about feminism at the same time in high school." I trusted Penny's judgment, especially because she knew so well what the center needed. She recommended my hiring Courtney. But she did have a concern. Her friends had told her that Courtney was sometimes unwilling to press her own opinions on others. "They said this was one of her best traits," she reported. "I agree that it's great to listen to others, but sometimes you have to take the lead. I hope Courtney can do that, too."

In fact, Penny's concern about Courtney was prescient. Although she had many of the characteristics needed to make the center work well, it turned out that Courtney was uncomfortable with the mentoring role the internship brought with it. Her problems in this regard stemmed from her view that learning was best done among equals. She had trouble deciding when to tell students who worked at the center what to do, and when to let them find their own way. If they made suggestions that were questionable, she felt it was not her place to discourage or even to provide guidance to them. But at the same time, when they failed to generate their own ideas, she could not hide her annoyance. Courtney resented the frequency with which students came to her for project suggestions. "We're equals. Why do they have to ask about every little thing?" she would question. I urged her to recognize that she was more experienced than the students and could legitimately act as their mentor. She should not simply assume that the students would be able to select the best projects or know how to carry them out by themselves.

Trouble began at the first meeting of the year when Courtney tried to get the seventeen student workers and volunteers to suggest projects for the semester. They responded by turning the question back to Courtney, asking what she had in mind, but she refused to answer. When no concrete suggestions were forthcoming by the end of the meeting, Courtney, clearly growing impatient, told the students that the center was theirs, and that it would surely fail unless they came up with new ideas for education and outreach. But the students continued only to offer vague generalities. "I want to work on relationships," said Gretchen. Barbara referred to her goal of "changing attitudes on campus," while Julie talked about "doing something about violence or child abuse." No matter how hard she tried, Courtney could not pin them down to anything more specific nor engage them in discussion of the benefits or disadvantages to the center of one program compared to another.

After the meeting, she was extremely distressed. "If we are going to be democratic," she told me, "I can't just tell them what to do. How will they ever learn if they don't take responsibility for themselves?" I tried to explain to Courtney that, for reasons I myself did not understand, my experience was that few students felt confident that they possessed the tools to plan and implement concrete projects from start to finish. That explained their reluctance to engage. They knew what they wanted to change—the sexist attitudes and actions they saw around them every day. But they did not know how to get others to think or act differently. They had no experience imagining how social change might actually occur. "You're using the wrong model," I suggested to Courtney. "It's not a democracy, but an apprenticeship. You're the one with the skills. You need to exercise leadership—to take the students through this, teaching them to plan, organize, and evaluate projects step by step."

Courtney had a hard time with this. She felt that doing as I suggested risked being disrespectful to the students. Instead she wanted to, as she put it, "empower the students by allowing them to take ownership of their projects." We revisited this issue over and over again. I would explain that the only way students could come to feel powerful was to be mentored. It was not disrespectful to offer them the support they needed to develop skills and confidence. For Courtney to give them responsibility for projects without providing them with the tools necessary for the task was in fact to disempower them, to deny them the space and time to learn what she already knew. She had to learn to teach, I insisted.

Slowly, Courtney's attitude began to change. Partly this was the result of our talks, but more it was a consequence of her own experience at the center. Ultimately, she learned the hard way. Several embarrassing program failures demonstrated, better than I could have, that she could not leave projects entirely up to the students. Invariably, when she failed to monitor a project closely, it fell apart. When that happened Courtney was left in the unenviable position of trying to pick up the pieces herself.

A turning point for her came in the third week of the semester, when one of the student assistants, Harriet, volunteered to organize a Brown Bag luncheon. She wanted to show a film featuring the a cappella women's singing group, Sweet Honey in the Rock. The day of the Brown Bag, with thirty students and faculty waiting at the center, not only had Harriet neglected to pick up the film, but she never came to the center or bothered to call. "I couldn't believe it," Courtney shouted over the phone to me later that afternoon when I had returned to campus from a meeting out of town. "There I was sitting at the center with the audience staring at me. I didn't think I had to go over every single little detail with her."

Courtney also learned that there were jobs and projects that needed to be done, such as putting up posters or greeting students who wandered into the center, that were regularly being neglected by the student assistants. At first Courtney tried to fill in the gaps by doing everything herself. However, it was soon obvious that the sheer volume of center programming required considerably more effort than she could provide alone—regardless of how well organized she was. Courtney finally had no choice but to exercise her authority and insist that student assistants follow through on the unpopular jobs, with or without their agreement. Most important in changing her attitude, however, was her discovery that when she neglected their supervision, some student assistants spent their entire work time sitting around the center talking to friends instead of working on their projects. "It's just not fair," she told me. "I hate to keep on the students all the time, but I'm not going to let them make a few people do all the work."

It was a different Courtney, who, near the end of the spring semester, told me of her decision to organize a welfare project and make the student assistants go door-to-door in the dorms. "This is important. There's so much apathy and misinformation about women and welfare. We can't reach the students unless we all pitch in. I know they aren't happy about it, but I did a training program to show them what to do. If they are still scared, they can go in pairs. But I told them everybody is going to do this, whether they want to or not."

I decided to hire Audrey, the intern who followed Courtney, when during her visit to Colgate she suggested holding a women's leadership conference on campus. She wanted to make the conference the centerpiece of her internship. She explained that it would be a great way to involve many Colgate women who had not previously participated in center activities: "Everyone wants to be a leader, so I think we'd have great attendance, and at the conference we can introduce them to feminist concepts and ideas. We could even invite students from other colleges to come." By the end of her interview, Audrey had convinced Courtney, the students, and me that a conference would be an exciting innovation. Courtney made us promise to invite her back to the campus to attend.

Organizing the conference the following year was an enormous undertaking, but Audrey and the students working with her pulled it off. Even more importantly, they managed to do so without short-changing the rest of the center's programming. Though it turned out to be too expensive and logistically difficult to expand attendance beyond Colgate, the on-campus conference was a great success. It became the first in a series of annual day-long leadership conferences sponsored by the center.

One of Audrey's priorities was to attract Colgate students who might otherwise not be interested in a women's studies event. She solicited names of campus leaders from deans, faculty, and student organizations. Each was sent a personal invitation to the conference that explained she had been nominated to participate in this unique opportunity because of her leadership potential. The invitation also made clear that those who accepted were expected to attend the entire conference. By emphasizing a rigorous selection process, complimenting their leadership ability, and insisting that they take the conference seriously if they decided to participate, Audrey succeeded in making attendance at the conference seem like a privilege. As one student expressed it: "My friends thought it was really cool I was asked."

I worked closely with Audrey to formulate goals for the conference. We agreed that exposing student leaders to the kinds of skills they would need to effectively organize others was important. We also wanted to be sure that the examples of organizing had feminist content. Our message would be that individual leadership skills could be put to collective use, in particular to promote the eradication of sexism. To this end, we invited a "campus educator" from the National Organization for Women (NOW) to facilitate the conference. Vanessa, the NOW representative, offered to run a hands-on workshop that would take students through the stages and tasks necessary for organizing a successful event.

After this all was settled, Audrey became uneasy that someone representing NOW might seem too radical to the cross section of Colgate students we hoped would attend the conference. "They've heard of NOW," Audrey worried, "but a lot of them don't know anything about it except the negative stuff they learn from the media. Maybe they'll be turned off." Despite her doubts, the NOW workshop sounded so exciting that we decided to go ahead with it. We hoped that students would be willing to look beyond labels, and we counted on Vanessa to win them over. "Even if some people are put off," I told Audrey, "it's worth it. We will have a chance to expose a hundred Colgate students to ideas they haven't heard before, and teach them something about NOW."

At the beginning of the conference, however, I looked around the room with trepidation as Vanessa announced to the assembled students that they were going to spend the day planning a simulated march on Washington protesting violence against lesbians. I knew there was homophobia at Colgate, and the women's studies program was stigmatized by many as the "dyke major." Now we were sponsoring a leadership conference that focused on homosexuality! I had no idea how the students would react. But Vanessa did not miss a step. She gave no one the time to have second thoughts. With a big smile on her face, she self-deprecatingly told the students: "I'm a middle-aged, overweight, African American lesbian. If I can organize people, you can, too. Let's go!"

Vanessa was a dynamo. She bustled among "subcommittees" of students, most of whom had never considered participating in a protest march, let alone one about homosexuality. She encouraged them, criticized them, and kept them focused on their task. "How are we going to get three hundred Colgate students to Washington and back?" she challenged students planning transportation. To the security subcommittee: "What do we do if fraternity guys try to harass students going to the march? What about if people in Washington try to stop us? We need a plan!" She had probing questions for the students working on media and publicity: "What's the best way to make sure every student on campus knows what is happening? How do we get them involved?" For those assigned to write a mission statement that could draw others in, she asked, "How do we explain, clearly and concisely, why it's important to stand up against violence against lesbians, and why people should support the march?" And for the committee formulating a plan to follow up and continue the work of the march, "What do we do when we come back to Colgate to make sure that the campus continues to be educated about this and other feminist issues? How do we exercise leadership here?"

When the committees had completed their work, Vanessa reassembled the conference participants for a reporting session. Each committee shared its plans, asking for and responding to suggestions and criticisms from others. The excitement in the room was palpable, and Vanessa orchestrated the scene like the pro she was. It was impossible to think of this only as an exercise.

When the conference ended, students lingered on, still engaged in arguing the finer points of renting buses or organizing carpools, of making phone calls or personal visits to local news media. The conference evaluation forms later confirmed what we already knew—the conference had been a huge success. Audrey was ecstatic when she read the student responses. "They loved it! They said that they had learned so much and had fun too. Lots of them want another conference next year, and a couple asked for information on actual marches they could attend. But the best was from someone named Weslea, who wrote, 'This is what class should be like thirty weeks a year!' "

Inevitably, there were students who did not share this enthusiasm. A few evaluations even indicated that participants were quite angry. They complained that the conference was not really about leadership. "I didn't hear the word leadership mentioned all day. I hate politics, and that's what this conference was really about," wrote one. Another was furious that she had not been told ahead of time "that this whole thing would end up being an exercise in propaganda for NOW. I would never go to a NOW march, especially with a bunch of lesbians." Audrey was deeply disturbed by these responses. But I told her that a handful of disgruntled participants was a small price to pay for an event that so many students had enjoyed and learned from. "We did exactly as advertised. The students spent the day thinking about leading in ways they had never done before."

During campus interviews with the next set of intern finalists the following spring, I asked each of them to explain how she might focus next year's leadership conference. I offered the internship to Nadia partially because she seemed so enthusiastic about the event and so clear in her suggestions for new themes. She wanted to incorporate discussions of her own interests in women's health care and sexuality. Especially because I knew I would be on leave in the fall, I wanted to hire someone like Nadia, who already had clear ideas of what she wanted to do. I hoped she would be able to replicate the success of the first conference, while avoiding the trap of simply repeating what we had already done.

Because of Nadia's interest in women's health and counseling, I had made a special effort, both during her interview and in discussions before the semester began, to clarify and emphasize the difference between a counseling center and the content of the Center for Women's Studies. These talks went well and I felt sure that she understood and agreed that the center's primary mission was not emotional support, but education.

Since I was on leave, I had only sporadic contact with Nadia during the fall semester. I did, however, continue to monitor the center's programming from afar, talking to students and faculty about how things were going. It was not long before I began to worry about the direction in which Nadia was taking the center. She was single-mindedly pushing the projects which interested her and neglecting the many others with which the center had come to be associated. That fall, the programs disproportionately emphasized psychological advice on sexuality, self-esteem, and personal empowerment.

Alarmed by the pattern that had emerged, I confronted Nadia when I returned from leave in December. Pointing out the problem of programmatic imbalance, I reminded her of our earlier discussions about the center's mission of education and outreach as opposed to psychological support. I also stressed once again how important it was for the center to address all of the different interests represented on campus. To my surprise, our discussion was not at all strained. Nadia assured me that she understood what I meant, and remarked that we could use the spring leadership conference to explore themes she now realized had been neglected.

However, when school resumed in January and we talked in detail about the conference, Nadia informed me that the planning had already been completed. Rather than inviting a guest speaker like Vanessa, Nadia and the student assistants had decided to organize the conference as a series of small workshops. By January, they had already received acceptances from several of Colgate's deans, from an intern in the Africana and Latin American studies program, and from two staff members from the campus counseling center, all of whom had been asked to act as facilitators. In addition, Nadia informed me, the conference committee had planned that I would deliver the keynote address at the beginning of the conference.

It was clear from even a cursory look at the program that this conference differed significantly from the last, but not in a way that I felt good about. Instead of an emphasis on social change, it had a decidedly self-help and psychological tone. Nadia's idea was that the leadership skills developed at the conference would help students in their personal lives and careers. My impression was that it was the kind of conference a corporation might run to motivate its employees to get along and get ahead. What it lacked was any discussion of the social or political uses to which such skills might be put, beyond those of personal career advancement or increasing individual self-esteem. I was not concerned that the topic of this second conference was different from the last; on the contrary, I had urged Nadia and the students to avoid repeating the first conference. But it was clear that despite her apparent understanding of my concern about an excessively psychological focus, Nadia's interests had carried the day. Furthermore, it was too late to do much about it.

But I did have the keynote address. I decided to use it, not to undermine, but to offset the self-help message of the conference. Though the conference had largely been stripped of any feminist content, I could raise these ideas once again, by emphasizing the collective uses to which individual leadership skills could be put. I asked the students to think of leadership not as an end in itself, but as a way to accomplish social goals in which they believed. For me, I explained, those goals were about bettering society in some way, and specifically about ending sexism. Others cared about different social problems. But the important point was not to see your leadership skills primarily as a way to facilitate your own success in an organization or career. At its best, being a leader was not an ego trip nor an attempt to show that you were more important than someone else. Real leaders, good leaders, are responsible for the uses to which they put their skills. I urged the students to learn to use the skills that the workshops would teach, but to understand them only as the first step, as tools. The really hard work was to figure out how to use those powerful tools to make others' lives better, not just their own.

Although my talk obviously did not alter the content of the conference, I hoped that it had succeeded in placing it in a broader context, one more consistent with the mission of the center and the women's studies program. At the wrap-up session, I was gratified to hear students returning to my questions concerning the purpose and goals of leadership. Several spoke eloquently about how they intended to use their skills to help other women, and they challenged other participants to do the same. Someone at least had gotten my message.

I knew in the aftermath of the conference that I would have to work closely with Nadia to get the center back on track. There were actually two separate issues that needed to be addressed: first, the programs and projects that the center would sponsor during the spring semester; and second, and at least as important, Nadia's own role vis-à-vis students at the center. As it turned out, changing the former was fairly simple, for Nadia was, as I had originally thought when I hired her, both intellectually curious and interested in an extensive variety of feminist issues. However, without anyone to push her in a different direction during the first semester, she had followed the path of least resistance. She had fallen back again and again on the issues of psychological counseling, sexuality, and health care with which she was most experienced and confident. Once I could talk with her every day and encourage her own eclecticism, she undertook a midcourse correction and restored a healthy balance to center programming.

Together, we had no trouble selecting projects for the spring semester that spoke to the varied interests of Colgate students.

But altering Nadia's relationship with the students proved considerably more difficult. During my absence in the first semester, Nadia had related to students more as a psychological counselor or close friend than as an educator or organizer. She had talked with them frequently and at length about their personal problems, especially sexuality, and had suggested to them what she thought of as solutions. She also had initiated and sat in on several center-sponsored psychological support groups, including those dealing with eating disorders, alcohol, and personal relationships.

When I resumed my duties in January, I told Nadia that her role as personal counselor had to end. She not only lacked the training necessary to ensure that the advice she offered students would not do them more harm than good, but, in addition, her time-consuming discussions with them distracted her from other work needed at the center. Under pressure, Nadia did make what I thought was a good-faith effort to alter the way she related to the students. But it was clear that she was doing so only because I insisted, not because I had convinced her that my approach was right. Indeed, though she never made it explicit, I knew that Nadia thought I was too rigid in limiting what she and the center did, and insensitive to the students' personal needs.

Halfway through the spring semester, however, Nadia herself came to reevaluate her role as an amateur analyst. She had become close friends the previous fall with Hillarie, a student assistant at the center. Nadia was Hillarie's counselor and confidante. They had spent many hours discussing Hillarie's confusion and ambivalence about whether she was a lesbian. Later, when Hillarie resolved her doubts, they talked at length about whether she should come out publicly as gay. But in the spring, after Hillarie had decided to come out, her relationship with Nadia changed. She no longer sought out Nadia for personal talks, and she rebuffed Nadia's efforts to continue to counsel her.

Tension between them grew and began to affect Nadia's work as well as that of the student assistants. It became particularly acute as organizing began on Hillarie's project—a campus celebration of homosexuality during "Be Glad" Week. Nadia reported to me that every suggestion she made was automatically rejected by Hillarie. Finally, just before the celebration, Hillarie blew up at a meeting of the "Be Glad" Week committee. She accused Nadia of "latent homophobia" and threatened to quit the center and take her friends with her. When Nadia demanded an explanation, Hillarie pointed to a poster on Nadia's office door that read: "I'm straight but not narrow." Hillarie angrily charged Nadia with putting up the poster in order to "prove her heterosexuality." Turning Nadia's own psychologizing against her, Hillarie claimed that Nadia subconsciously needed to show she was straight, especially because of her strong and public support of gay students on campus.

I first learned of all of this when Nadia, terribly upset, came to me for advice. "If it means so much to her, I'll take the poster down," she said, "but this is obviously about more than a poster. At the meeting, Hillarie went ballistic—she was screaming at me, and not even listening when I tried to explain." Nadia was sure that Hillarie's attack on her was related to their talks about sexuality. "I think she is embarrassed about having revealed her doubts to me, and resents that she needed help," explained Nadia.

Beyond her personal hurt, what really bothered Nadia was that her counseling relationship with Hillarie had come to threaten the functioning of the center. Nadia admitted that her own inexperience and lack of training had contributed to creating the problem. "I was only trying to help," she told me, "but I guess that's not really enough. I had no idea it could backfire like this."

In the end, Hillarie did decide to remain part of the center. But her continued tense and distrustful attitude toward Nadia cast a pall over the center's work for the remainder of the semester. Nadia, for her part, seemed to have learned her lesson. For her own reasons, not just because of my instructions, she was much more careful about involving herself in the personal lives and problems of the students. Instead, she found satisfaction in concentrating on what the center had been set up to do—stretching students' minds and challenging their intellect.

At the end of the center's third year I was again faced with the daunting task of selecting among a strong pool of intern finalists. In the end, however, one candidate's story of how she took the initiative to organize on her campus set her apart. In her interview, Melanie explained that soon after declaring herself a history major, she realized that there were no plans to commemorate Women's History Month at her college the following spring. "I approached several faculty and lots of other students about whether they would help organize a celebration. Everyone told me what a terrible shame it was that nothing had been done, but literally no one offered to do anything." Melanie decided to do it herself. "She is a born organizer," wrote one professor in her recommendation. "By sheer will, Melanie managed to bring almost the whole college together to celebrate feminist and women's history. It was unbelievable!" It sounded as if Melanie were made for the women's studies internship.

At the interview, Melanie also talked excitedly about how her campus women's history celebrations had incorporated a universalistic perspective. She had made a special effort, she reported, to include programs and displays exploring the history of women of color and highlighting the ways their experiences intersected those of white women and other marginalized groups. I was therefore not surprised that I touched a nerve when I asked Melanie whether she thought that, as a women's studies intern, she might be helpful in resolving the tensions and divisions among African American, white, Latina, and Asian women students on Colgate's campus. Without the slightest hesitation, Melanie responded, "That's really something I could put my heart and soul into."

But Melanie's goal was to prove much harder to achieve than she had foreseen. I was aware of the difficulties ahead of her because I had experienced the depths of the divisions existing among students. Nonetheless, when she arrived on campus, I encouraged her to take on this issue as one of her major priorities. The problem was that despite the efforts of previous interns, few if any African American or Latina students attended center workshops or discussions, including those specifically dealing with racism, affirmative action, Latin culture, or black history. In spite of Melanie's enthusiasm and hard work, this pattern continued into the fall, and she grew increasingly frustrated: "What's the use of discussing racism if the students of color won't come? They say that it's not their responsibility to teach whites about their racism. That's just like feminists who say that they shouldn't have to explain sexism to men who don't get it. But ending sexism and racism is everybody's problem—it just won't happen unless we all talk about it together." I of course agreed with Melanie, and the center continued to put on programs concerning women and race relations and to highlight the contributions of women of many backgrounds, even if, as often occurred, the only students who attended were white. Melanie, however, had difficulty fighting the feeling that she was failing. "I know it's great for the students who do show up, but is it ever frustrating to keep trying to get a dialogue going when students of color stay away."

Then, in quick succession, three separate incidents made Melanie's job with regard to a cross-ethnic dialogue that much more difficult. Two of these involved me personally, and the third focused on one of the center's student assistants. Their cumulative effect was that women's studies incurred the wrath of some of the most vocal African American students on campus.

The first occurred as the result of a discussion in the women's studies senior seminar I was teaching in the fall. One day in class, my students were maintaining—as they frequently did—that the situation of women in the United States was worse today than in the recent past. To illustrate this claim, one student, Linda, made an analogy to racism: "It's just like with racism in how it works. Prejudice and discrimination against women and African Americans are much more subtle today. People want to think that they aren't racist or sexist, so they don't always do it in an obvious way, and that's what makes it worse." Several others agreed. "Linda's right. There is more sexism today than before," Lydia declared. "Of course, you can't always actually see it, but you know it's there whenever women are around men. That's why it's tough to fight."

I listened, amazed yet again at what I had heard so many times. These arguments made no sense to me: that racism and sexism were always present whether they were recognizable or not; that the more subtle prejudice or discrimination was, the worse it was; and that there were no effective mechanisms available for women to combat sexism. Even more difficult to grasp was my students' continued pessimism even after we had studied polls that demonstrated a sharp decline in prejudice against both women and African Americans. Their response had been that the polls only indicated that Americans were better at hiding their prejudiced feelings now than in the past.

On this particular day in class, I made explicit my strong disagreement with this point of view that denied both the fact and the possibility of change. I provided examples of vicious forms of prejudice and discrimination in the past that had all but been eliminated today. I cited the terrible history of legal segregation and the lynching of African Americans in the South after Emancipation, the violent resistance to granting civil and voting rights to the black population, the fact that women could not vote until 1920, that birth control had long been illegal, and that until the 1950s, pregnant or married women were routinely denied jobs and excluded from jury duty.

I also noted positive changes that had affected many people in both groups. I mentioned the growth of an increasingly prosperous and well-educated middle-class African American population, the election of African American politicians in significant numbers, women's increased control over reproduction, and the fact that because women had jobs and their own income, they had a better chance of getting out of violent or unhappy marriages. "All this is new," I told them. "There's still plenty that is wrong and unfair. Discrimination and prejudice still exist. But change is possible. It's real, and it happened because people fought injustice—both subtle and obvious—and refused to be discouraged or give up."

What this seminar most revealed to me was the gaping chasm between the attitudes of my generation of activists and those of my students. It was almost visceral. In the face of overwhelming sexism and racism, activists of the 1960s were hopeful, optimistic that we could somehow create a better world. We saw the possibility of progress, though we knew achieving it would be difficult. In contrast, my students felt helpless and politically impotent when confronted by the injustice around them. They exaggerated its power and reacted with despair.

As I mused on this situation, little did I know that others were also thinking—and talking—about the class. Early the following week, Bettina, an African American student I knew well, stopped me on campus to ask why I had claimed that racism no longer existed in the United States. "I didn't say that. I don't believe it," I replied, astonished. Bettina paused for just a minute before retorting, "Then why is everyone talking about how you told your senior seminar that African Americans have no problems today because racism is dead?"

The first thing I did at next Monday's seminar was to address explicitly the misinterpretation that Bettina had alerted me to. However, it was of course too late; the damage had already been done. Rumors fly on college campuses, and as far as the Colgate student body was concerned, Professor Mandle did not believe that racism was present in the United States. Many students were disappointed and angry not only with me but also with women's studies.

As if this were not bad enough, the seminar incident became connected to a second and more serious controversy. This one centered on a proposal that one dormitory, a theme house named Harlem Renaissance Center (HRC), be exempt from the college's new policy requiring all first-year students to live in first-years-only dormitories. HRC was described in the college catalog as "a close-knit community [that] promotes the culture and heritage of people of African descent." Since students living in HRC were almost exclusively black, it constituted a de facto separate African American residence on campus. I was part of a committee appointed by the dean to decide the controversial question of whether HRC should be allowed to house first-year students. In effect we were being asked whether the school should, for African Americans alone, make an exception concerning its rules for first-year students.

The committee included several students, four administrators, and another faculty member in addition to myself. We wrangled for months but failed to reach a consensus. Ultimately we delivered a report to the president summarizing arguments both for and against an HRC exemption. The strongest advocates for the exemption argued that only HRC as presently constituted could provide African American first-year students with the "comfortable and supportive environment" they needed if they were to succeed at Colgate. Life in conventional first-year dormitories, one administrator admonished us, "would be torture for first-year African American students, with no one to talk to or help them out."

There were others on the committee, however, including myself, who argued strenuously against an exemption. In contrast to HRC residents and their advocates on the committee who eagerly made their opinions public, opponents of having first-years at HRC, aside from myself, were not willing to defend their views publicly. They refused to be forthcoming about the arguments they had made in the committee. I considered this self-imposed silence to be hypocritical. Furthermore, I thought that in censoring themselves, these faculty and students were denying the campus a full airing of an important issue.

Therefore, when the student newspaper asked for my opinion on the HRC exemption, I carefully explained the position I had taken in the committee. I told them that I believed in the wisdom of Colgate's policy that all first-years should reside together. It was important that students of the same graduating class have common experiences together. That required them to meet and live with first-years of different backgrounds, interests, abilities, and hobbies—for at least their first year. The college, I continued, had a responsibility to smooth the transition from high school by providing, in all first-year dorms, a well-trained and supportive network of advisors, counselors, and ombudspeople. This support network would be there to help all first-years with the difficult problems that adjusting to college inevitably entailed. Finally, I argued that the separation of African American students from others from the moment they set foot on campus set up patterns of segregation—albeit voluntary ones—that socially, intellectually, and personally were extremely harmful to the African American students involved.

No sooner did the article outlining my views appear in the student newspaper than I was beset by questions from many of my students. Confused and in some cases incensed, they wanted to know why I was "taking a position against the African American students on campus." Other students, however, did not even bother to talk to me, already convinced that I was an out-and-out racist. Their anger was exacerbated because of the earlier rumors from the senior seminar, and because, as the only opponent who was willing to speak out publicly, I was thought to be the sole committee member who had adopted that position.

The worst moment for me came when an assistant dean, a friend who had not been on the committee, asked me to lunch and with tears in her eyes pleaded with me to change my position. "I hate to think of you as a racist," she said. "I know that you have worked for justice all your life. But what can I think when you fight against the African American students who want to live by themselves?" When I was too astonished to reply immediately, she went on, "I hate it, but I really believe it's racist to resist separation. It seems like the only real answer to today's tensions." Hearing her words, I recognized the full dimensions of my problem. I had been misinterpreted when I argued in my seminar that it was possible to reduce racism and sexism. I had compounded this difficulty by refusing to censor myself regarding HRC and by speaking out in favor of what I believed to be not only right in principle, but also in the best interests of all Colgate students. And now I was thought to be a racist because, of all things, I opposed segregation.

The third negative incident that semester involving women's studies and students of color concerned Tracy, a student assistant. As part of her project at the center, Tracy had chosen to submit biweekly articles to the student newspaper on subjects related to women and feminism. As a double major in women's studies and Africana and Latin American studies, her columns frequently addressed racial issues too. Shortly after the 1996 Million Man March in Washington, D.C., she wrote an article criticizing the march's policy of excluding women. Calling on her knowledge of black history, she traced the importance of African American women's contributions to civil rights and other struggles for justice. She reported that African American women leaders had recently spoken out against their exclusion from the march, calling it sexist and discriminatory. Tracy concluded by agreeing with these women that the march's policy indicated a disturbing unwillingness to accept women as equals.

Soon after her article appeared, Tracy came to talk to Melanie and me. Describing the overwhelmingly negative reaction to her article from students and even some faculty, Tracy worried that her outspokenness would harm women's studies. "I feel terrible," she told us. "I guess maybe I shouldn't have written what I did, but it seemed so wrong to me that women were barred from that march." According to Tracy, most people were outraged that she had written about an event that concerned African Americans. "Both my black and my white friends asked me why I, a white person, thought that I had the right to judge people who aren't white. They said at least I should have checked to see if it was okay with the African American women on campus."

Tracy also mentioned that one of her professors was "really upset" at her for criticizing African Americans. His position, according to Tracy, was that African Americans have had such a hard time that, even if she was right in this case, she shouldn't add to their problems by being critical, regardless of the circumstances. Tracy turned apologetically to Melanie. "I know how hard you've tried to build strong bonds with all the different groups on campus," she said unhappily. "I really hope I haven't ruined things for you by making people think women's studies is racist."

It was true that Melanie had borne much of the hostility that I had inadvertently triggered, and now she was facing yet another obstacle to her efforts to reach students of color. But Melanie rose to the occasion. "You don't have to apologize to me or anyone else," she told Tracy. "You didn't do anything wrong. If you believe it's wrong to exclude women, you should say so. If feminists had shut up because they were afraid they might offend somebody or other, nothing would have ever changed. You don't need permission to offer an opinion about something you care about. All you need is guts! We'll just deal with the fallout, that's all." I could not have been more proud of her.

For the remainder of the year, Melanie characteristically refused to concede defeat: "It just means I have more work to do to build the trust that we need to all work together." Melanie's achievements that year fell far short of what she had hoped to accomplish in resolving the tensions that had driven a wedge between women of color and the center. But she had persisted in doing what I asked of her; in the face of rebuffs and disappointments she had constantly asserted that the center and women's studies was there for everyone.

Gwen, the last intern I hired, arrived at Colgate with high expectations, but became increasingly disappointed that the student assistants and those who attended the center's programs were less feminist and politically sophisticated than she had anticipated. After only a month, she vented her frustration to me: "I spent my last two years in college being patient with people who weren't sure they 'really' were feminists, or who stood on the sidelines and didn't want to get involved. Sometimes I feel I can't take the apathy anymore. I just want to shake someone!"

In an attempt to increase political interest among the students, Gwen created a center series she called "Standing Up for Your Beliefs." It brought feminist activists to campus to talk about reproductive choice, antidiscrimination legislation, welfare reform, and gay rights. After each presentation, Gwen urged the students to create projects to "Take Action." She encouraged them to get involved in signing petitions, writing letters to legislators, and sharing pamphlets and information with the campus as a whole. While most of the center students liked and respected Gwen's efforts, several complained to me that she was too often impatient and demanding. At a staff meeting later in the semester, these feelings finally came to a boil. Gwen was in the midst of critiquing another student assistant's project idea when Annie spoke up: "You know Gwen, not everything has to be perfectly feminist or political to be important. Why can't we just have some programs that are fun? It's like you want everyone to be a radical feminist right away. You need to lighten up!"

Gwen was devastated by Annie's remark. Until then Gwen had not realized that a tug-of-war had developed between her and those students who did not share her urgency to articulate a feminist politics. I myself felt torn, for I admired Gwen's intensity and passionate concern. In fact, many of the students were far too apathetic for my taste, too. But I also knew that the center would succeed only if it was responsive to the students' own level of feminist consciousness. "We can educate and challenge them," I told Gwen, "but only gently."

After the incident with Annie, Gwen worked hard at harnessing her impatience. She generally succeeded, but the following spring another incident showed that she still had much to learn. Several student assistants had developed an exciting project in conjunction with a teacher from a local high school. The teacher had called me to ask for help with a group of her female students. They were from troubled homes, all had low aspirations and self-esteem, and several were in abusive relationships with boyfriends; the teacher was worried about their becoming pregnant. "I heard about the center," she said, "I thought maybe some women's studies students from Colgate could come over and just talk to them." Two weeks later, and once a week after that during the rest of the school year, students from the center met at the high school with a dozen or so girls. They talked about each others' lives, their goals, their relationships, and their futures. Few of these girls had ever met a college student before and they all found the discussions exciting. They eagerly looked forward to the weekly meetings, and for their part, the Colgate students loved the project, which put them in touch with a world they knew little about.

Seeing its success, Gwen decided to expand the outreach to high schools by bringing a larger group of girls from several additional schools to Colgate for a full day. She and several student assistants worked to plan a "Move Up Day" that would introduce the visitors to college life, women's studies, and the center. The intention was to provide a mix of fun and information for the forty-five high schoolers.

The day seemed to go well, but a week later when Gwen had read the "Move Up Day" evaluation forms she learned that it had not gone quite as smoothly as we believed. While most of the high school girls were enthusiastic about the visit, a significant number expressed dissatisfaction with one part of the program. They didn't like the workshop that Gwen had run in the afternoon. In it, she had talked about women and advertising while each student made a collage out of advertisements from women's magazines.

Gwen's goals for the session had been two. First, she wanted to try to raise the consciousness of the students concerning the way women's bodies are used by the media to sell products. And second, she hoped to make them aware of the media-induced pressure on women to buy products in order to be beautiful. The collage making was fine—the students thought it was fun. But the discussion backfired. According to the evaluation forms, many of the students resented Gwen's attempts to make feminist points. "I don't see why she's so against these advertisements," wrote one high school girl. "I think the models are cool." Another echoed this view: "I didn't like how she tried to push us into her ideas. It sounded like she was trying to say the magazines were bad, but they're not. The program shouldn't be so negative—women aren't being treated as savages or animals or anything like that." A third student had an alternative suggestion: "I'd like to hear more about women's traditional roles that have carried over from the past. Not everyone wants to be a feminist you know."

It was pretty clear that in trying to warn these students about bulimia, anorexia, and women's sexual objectification, Gwen had come on too strong. Instead of becoming interested in feminist ideas, at least some of these girls, hearing them for the first time, thought they were weird, incomprehensible, or just plain wrong. When Gwen read the evaluations, she was mortified that she had again pushed too hard. "I thought since we only had them for one day, we better make use of it," she explained. "There was so much I wanted to tell them, I couldn't decide what to leave out. It sounds like I scared them to death. When am I ever going to learn?"

But in fact Gwen was learning all the time. Indeed, watching her and the interns before her learn and grow and change throughout their internships was one of the best parts of my job. I treasured the opportunity to mentor these young women, to experience with them how difficult and frustrating, exciting and gratifying it is to help others to discover and explore women's studies and feminism. Although each year I was tortured by the fear that I would never again find the kind of intern I needed, each one, though different, in her own way made a mark. We were a team. I gave them the freedom and support they needed to do an extremely demanding and difficult job. In their turn, they rewarded me with a vital and thriving center to which students were drawn by its openness, its tolerance, and its intellectual excitement.

CHAPTER 3

The Classes

The center and the women's studies program were interdependent. To the extent that the center's outreach was successful, it was likely that more students and faculty would be interested in taking or teaching women's studies classes. At the same time, more women's studies courses with higher enrollments would feed the center's programming. The two together could be powerful. If successful, they could change the tone of the campus.

Each semester I taught the introductory class in women's studies myself. Because so many students take no more than an introductory course in this field, its content is of critical importance. Typically it will be their only opportunity to rigorously examine feminist scholarship. As a result, I organized the course to explore the spectrum of feminist thought and its practical application to the issues that women face in their everyday lives.

Soon after I began teaching this course, however, I realized that the students were reluctant to explore all sides of the issues under examination. They were altogether too eager to settle for what they thought of as the "feminist" position, without adequately examining alternative arguments or views. My uneasiness in this regard was heightened after speaking with Carey, a senior who had enrolled in the class because, as she put it, "I didn't think I should graduate and go out into the world without at least taking one women's studies course." Several weeks into the semester, Carey had come to my office because she was concerned that her failure to participate in class discussions might hurt her grade. I told Carey she was right; her grade would suffer if she did not involve herself more. But I also mentioned how puzzled I was by her silence. I told her I expected more from someone whose tests and written work were so consistently intelligent and well written and who was older and more mature than many of the other students. At first Carey was reluctant to reply, but as we talked she finally admitted that she hesitated to participate in class because she felt "intimidated" by students who seemed to be "more feminist." Carey continued softly, "I find that I don't always agree with the feminist position, but I don't want to look like a sexist. I would rather keep quiet than pretend I agree with them." She said there were others in the class with whom she had spoken who felt similarly. Even some of those who openly sided with feminist orthodoxy had told her that they were not saying what they really thought, but were "just going along."

Carey's comments confirmed my own growing suspicions that my students were censoring themselves. They either failed to speak at all, or, when they did, they sought to align their views with what they believed other students—or even perhaps myself—thought was "really feminist." I asked Carey whether anyone had explicitly tried to discourage her from speaking her mind. "No, not really," she replied. "But I know what they're thinking."

I was truly shocked that my own efforts to create an open atmosphere in my classroom had been so unsuccessful. I immediately queried Carey about whether there was something in my teaching style that was responsible for this pressure to conform. Her response revealed that I had missed the point. I was not the problem. "Oh, I know you're always trying to get us to say what we really think, telling us that there isn't just one view that's feminist. But who's going to admit in a women's studies class that she has questions about abortion? It's embarrassing to seem politically backward in front of your friends." The "chilly climate" that many feminists argue is present for female students, and especially for feminists, on college campuses had come home to roost! Despite my best efforts, in my own classroom there existed an atmosphere that discouraged students from expressing their real ideas and views.

The problem for me was to find a better way to encourage the expression of fresh thinking by my students. I could of course engage in more exhortation. But as Carey's comments revealed, my efforts in that direction already had little effect. Instead, I devised a plan that, although far from a complete solution, I thought at least might help. For each of the series of controversial issues about which the class read extensively, I randomly assigned students to prepare to argue a position in class. The students did not get to choose which side they were on: for or against legalized abortion; in favor of or against banning pornography; rejecting or advocating single-sex educational institutions.

Needless to say, many of the students forced to adopt what they thought was the "antifeminist" position raised an immediate outcry. They objected to being required to defend something that they feared would make them look ridiculous. "I have to switch," demanded Faith after a class in which I had assigned her the task of defending pornography on free-speech grounds. "I hate pornography. There's no way that I can argue that it should be allowed." Beth was close behind her. "I was an intern for Planned Parenthood last summer," she announced. "Can you seriously expect me to defend an antiabortion position?" Their emotional reaction only reinforced my conviction that they were reluctant to think deeply about views that deviated from conventional feminist wisdom. I continued therefore to insist on the exercise. What was at issue was to me elementary, but to my students a totally new idea: in order to figure out for themselves what they thought about a particular issue, they needed to know and understand all points of view—including those they ultimately rejected.

Despite their vociferous objections, my forcing dialogue in this way created fascinating classes. It was not just the debates themselves that were informative and lively. Even more so were the discussions that followed. They were more nuanced and thoughtful than those I had grown accustomed to hearing, with a surprising diversity present in the points of view expressed. My new format seemed to help students to hear that there was at least some plausibility in views that they had earlier tended simply to dismiss as nonfeminist. With this the case, it became easier for them to risk articulating previously unthinkable thoughts.

Some of the most interesting were those classes concerned with sexual relations, an issue with which feminists have long been concerned, and about which students tended to feel strongly. In one discussion, the class examined a policy on sexual relations and sexual assault developed at Antioch College in the early 1990s. This policy had stirred considerable national controversy when it was introduced. Its most unusual aspect was the requirement of explicit verbal agreement at each stage of sexual contact between students. Not surprisingly, it was about this issue that my students became most animated and engaged.

The debate itself was quite straightforward. The students assigned to argue that the policy should be adopted at Colgate marshaled national evidence to try to demonstrate that an unacceptably high incidence of sexual assault and date rape occurred on college campuses. They did research on sexual assault at Colgate and presented these data, too. They conducted interviews about the subject with various friends, administrators, and campus safety officials and reported the results in class. They argued that in the absence of a policy like Antioch's, there would be insufficient communication between students engaged in sexual activity. Without clear communication, they claimed, too many students were subtly or not-so-subtly pressured into engaging in unwanted sexual relations. If a set of rules similar to Antioch's were implemented at Colgate, they concluded, it would encourage verbal communication between sexual partners and thereby reduce the problem of date rape.

Those who opposed the policy usually took one of two tacks. Frequently, they tried to demonstrate that the policy in fact was unenforceable because its components—verbal agreement, stages of sexual contact—were poorly defined. In making the case against the policy, Phyllis pointed out: "If the guy wasn't giving consent but the girl thought he was, how can she be punished? It's a question of communication and his word against hers." The other recurring argument against the policy took exception to legislating sexual interaction in the name of trying to protect partners from one another. Except in cases of overt physical coercion that are of course illegal, this position argued that partners should be allowed to negotiate their own relationship without a set of standardized rules. Such rules, it was maintained, not only infringed on but actually violated individual privacy.

The open discussion that followed these presentations was always intense. Difficult and important questions were being raised. What constitutes legitimate evidence? Should universities have different rules and standards of conduct than the rest of the society? Are universities acting illegitimately *in loco parentis* when they try to shape students' personal relationships? Is this policy really gender neutral or does it tend, with respect to sexuality, to infantilize women and demonize men?

In class, debate was heated but resolution was rare. Students were often frustrated that no definitive answers were arrived at. From my point of view, however, these discussions were very useful. Students got to hear and take seriously points of view they had never considered, and they seemed more willing to express their own views. The format of a forced debate helped them to recognize that differences of opinion—intellectual conflict—were not just legitimate but even exhilarating.

Frequently in these sessions and especially during the Antioch debates, discussion veered off onto the tangent of the problem-ridden nature of the students' own personal relationships. The women in my classes consistently used words like "terrible," "dysfunctional," "nonexistent," or "totally exploitative" to refer to their relationships with men. In explanation, they recounted a dreary litany of drunken campus parties at fraternities and elsewhere, humiliating one-night sexual "hook-ups," and testy, untrusting, and adversarial "relationships" in which there was hardly even an effort at communication. If I had allowed it, they would have turned almost every class into a discussion of the Colgate social scene.

It was difficult not to empathize with their distress and confusion. But while not wanting to ignore their concerns, I would not let my classes deteriorate into personal gripe sessions. Not only would I, and ultimately they, too, find such sessions excruciatingly boring, but even more important, such discussion would not help students to develop the skills they needed in order to really understand the situation they were in. Instead, I insisted that they address the broader social issues that both the Antioch policy and the Colgate social scene raised—the need for an analysis of male-female relations as a social problem.

In class, we approached this subject as we would any other complex social phenomenon: What are the contributing factors? Are there social trends likely to exacerbate or reduce this problem in the future? What are its consequences for social institutions like the family or the educational system? By assigning academic readings on these subjects, I taught that their personal problems could be placed in a social context. In this way I tried to provide them with the tools of sociological analysis.

Though I was able to limit the extent to which personal relationships were discussed in class, they nevertheless were the substance of much talk at the center. Even I occasionally was drawn into these discussions. The salience of personal relationships did not surprise me. Young adults could be expected to be preoccupied with intimate relationships, especially in situations where so many of them were unsatisfactory. But what did repeatedly worry me was how helpless, even paralyzed, these students felt concerning their ability to avoid sexually unpleasant or exploitative relationships. Even less did they seem to have any idea how to build healthy, mutually satisfactory ones.

Their concerns were obviously real and important, but as with my classes, I wanted to avoid having the center become excessively focused on personal problems. Women's Coalition, a student-led group that met weekly at the center, already provided a context where students could talk about personal issues in a supportive environment. What I wanted the center to do was to move students beyond themselves, to focus on women and gender not therapeutically but intellectually, understanding them as social issues with implications for social policy. To me, center-sponsored activities were opportunities to help students see that the source of their own problematic relationships went well beyond issues of individual psyches, preferences, or experiences. Their relationships, like those of others, were socially constructed and were therefore also subject to change.

But their feelings of passivity and despair, running like a thread through their conversations, continued to disturb me. These otherwise bright, assertive, and accomplished young women seemed to crumble when faced with the problem of trying to alter the nature of their intimate relations with men. Believing that relationships inevitably must victimize women, they had in effect just given up.

I thought one way to address this issue might be to invite to the center someone who would be able to analyze ways to prevent dysfunctional relationships. The person I chose to do so was Sandra Bellum, the director of a nearby rape crisis center. In her remarks at the well-attended Brown Bag session, Bellum emphasized the link between dysfunctional relationships and date rape—explaining how both could be prevented. She stressed the importance of working to change sexual attitudes and behavior, not only men's but also women's. To everyone's surprise, in turning to date rape, she announced that she was not going to discuss men at all. "Instead," she told us, "I want to direct my remarks to the women in the room. You are the ones who hold the key to preventing date rape."

Sandra warned the students that to think that women were inevitably victims in sexual encounters was to concede defeat. On the contrary, she maintained, women did not need to be victims. Citing the high incidence of alcohol use in instances of date rape, she urged the women who were present to take responsibility for themselves by not drinking in situations where sexual assault might be a risk. "You can help stop this problem if you just use common sense," she said. "Tell your friends. That's how each one of you can contribute to feminist social change and the decrease of date rape."

The students erupted in anger. Stacy jumped to her feet: "You're saying that women are responsible for rape. There's no way! If a man rapes me, it's his responsibility, not mine. I should be able to wear whatever I want, and do whatever I want—including getting drunk or walking naked down the street—without worrying about what some man might do to me." Other students agreed, accusing Sandra of blaming victims for their victimization. But Sandra was prepared; she obviously had considerable experience with just this reaction. She went right back at the students: "The whole point is that you don't have to be passive victims. You can decide what kind of relationships you have with men. Stop worrying about who is popular, who is cool. If college women didn't attend fraternity drinking parties, fraternities would change; if you demanded communicative relationships with college men, not hook-ups, men would have to respond. If a man hits or sexually assaults or rapes a woman, he is the guilty party. But I see cases of date rape all the time that could have been prevented by the woman's having the guts right from the start to insist on having a role in where they go, what they drink, and what they do."

There was silence in the room when Sandra finished. As if to avoid her, the students rushed off to class. I could see that Sandra had been shaken by the exchange. She told me that these confrontations were always very painful for her, especially because, as was frequently the case, it was other feminists who were the most furious at her remarks. "But then I remember the girls I see every day at my office who have been so deeply hurt, and I know I need to explain to women the ways that, in some situations at least, they can have more control. What good will it do if I just keep repeating that men are wrong? That's all too obvious," she said quietly.

For weeks after that Brown Bag discussion, conversations at the center swirled around the relationship between feminism and sexuality. The discussions mirrored the disagreements that have polarized feminists since the beginning of the second wave. One tendency within feminism has been to claim that a primary goal of the women's movement is to liberate women's sexuality and end the double standard that has existed between women and men. In contrast are the many feminist writers and activists who see sexuality as fraught with special danger for women. They warn women of the dire consequences that accompany heterosexual sex, and of the dangers of rape and unwanted pregnancy.

It is not only feminists who send contradictory messages about sex. It is difficult for students to know what to think or do surrounded by a culture that at once encourages them to be sexually liberated and at the same time constantly reminds them of lurking dangers. First-year orientations at most colleges and universities also reflect these contradictions. Workshops present new college students with a series of frightening admonitions about sexual assault and sexually transmitted diseases, including AIDS. But the same administrators and deans who do so, simultaneously refuse to act against the excessive alcohol consumption on campus that poisons students' sexual relations.

It is difficult for college women to sort out the messages about sexuality they are receiving. When I talk with my students about these issues, they often ask me what the feminist position is. I respond by reporting on the disagreements that exist, and offer my own view that neither "side," taken by itself, is right. Rather, I explain, some kind of responsible middle ground needs to be found. Women, like men, should have the ability to freely choose how they express their sexuality; yet that freedom is not absolute. Sexuality needs to be, like other activities we engage in, responsibly thought through and guided toward goals that we select for ourselves. Feminist activism has expanded the choices women can make, I tell them, but each individual woman has to consciously make her own sexual choices and then live with the consequences.

In my introductory women's studies course there were other classroom debates in which sexuality was also central. Two concerned pornography and sexual harassment. The first took up the issue of banning pornography. Those students assigned to construct arguments in favor of a ban typically did so by maintaining that the demeaning nature of pornography significantly harms women. It does so by creating and reinforcing negative stereotypes according to which women are viewed exclusively as sex objects, victimized by men. But often the students went further, quoting with approval Catherine MacKinnon's assertion that pornography is actually a form of violence. Asserting that words are acts, MacKinnon argues that pornography should, like other forms of physical violence, be legally prohibited. The students followed her lead and concluded that a ban was therefore justified.[1]

On the other side of the debate, while rarely defending pornography itself, students rejected censorship on a number of grounds. One was their discovery that many feminists and lesbians consume various kinds of pornography. Some feminists therefore maintain that viewing pornography is a form of sexual liberation. Other feminist opponents of a ban make a different argument. They stress that legally prohibiting pornography is dangerous for women because it threatens free speech. In class, students often noted that the historical suppression of birth control information was carried out in the name of protecting society from pornography. They also pointed out the frequency with which lesbian publications have been subjected to the same form of attack.

Regardless of their debate assignment, in class discussion virtually every student expressed hostility to pornography. But the debate format nevertheless succeeded in sensitizing them to the problems asso-

---

1. Catharine A. MacKinnon, *Only Words* (Cambridge: Harvard University Press, 1993).

ciated with censorship. Unlike previous classes on the subject, where banning was unanimously endorsed without so much as a dissenting voice, the give-and-take of the debate resulted in a smaller proportion of students enthusiastically favoring a total ban. Moreover, they were willing to seriously consider other possible methods of reducing the use of pornography. This was women's studies at its best: students grappling with an important and complex issue without trying to overly simplify it or rely only on a visceral response.

A similar engagement occurred when students debated whether, as I presented the issue, sexual harassment laws have "gone too far." Students assigned to support current sexual harassment legislation based their argument on the large number of cases in which the courts have found egregious sexual harassment in the workplace. This showed, they said, the need for laws to protect employees from employers and from others demanding sexual favors. Because I had assigned Colgate's own policy on sexual harassment as part of the course reading, these students also addressed the school's policy, warning of the dangers of sexual harassment of students by professors. They maintained that strong laws are needed to thwart professors who might be sexual predators.

In contrast, those assigned to oppose the implementation of the present law argued that it had already gone too far. Pointing to what they claimed were false accusations, these students raised free-speech issues similar to those explored in the discussion of pornography. They argued that overly zealous sexual harassment laws threaten free speech and academic freedom at universities.

Like pornography, sexual harassment was an issue that always drew a strong response from students. They were particularly concerned about their own vulnerability to potential harassers. As a result, in post-debate discussion, there was never anyone who took the position that sexual harassment should be tolerated. There were differences among them, however, in defining what constituted harassing behavior, and they struggled with this difficult question of definition.

The following exchange took place one day in class as students grappled with the reading they had done on the meaning of a hostile environment:

Pat: I'm the only one who can possibly know what makes me feel uncomfortable in class. If I say that I feel sexually harassed by a discussion, say, of a novel or of prostitution, then it should stop.

Rika: But that's impossible! If everyone who got uncomfortable or offended could end a discussion, no one would be able to talk anymore. I know there have to be some standards of what is maybe too much, but we have to be able to discuss things. What if you think a professor looks at you funny and you think that's sexual harassment, but if he looks at me the same way and I don't. Which is it?

Pat: Okay, but who gets to decide? No one has ever listened to women about this.

As in the Antioch sex code and the pornography debates, students often became frustrated that the problem of sexual harassment was not amenable to an easy solution. But their agreeing on a solution was not my objective. I wanted these classes, during which all sides received a hearing, to show the range of opinion possible on these issues, both within the society generally and among feminists. Forced to read about and confront conflicting views on pornography and sexual harassment, my students often acknowledged that before participating in these staged debates, their strong opinions had actually been based on little understanding or knowledge of these concepts and the laws regulating them.

It was not only students who had difficulty engaging in rational discussion about sexual harassment and pornography. When the director of Colgate's art gallery brought an exhibit of a famous photographer to campus, controversy erupted among the faculty and administration. I had thought my students' difficulty in sustaining a reflective attitude could be explained by their youth. But the experience of this show made it painfully clear that even university professors, trained in and committed to the process of rational dialogue, were capable of adopting positions based fundamentally on emotion.

A phone call from the provost's office first alerted me to the presence of the exhibit and the problems emerging from it. The provost explained that one of the secretaries in the department of art history was demanding the removal of the exhibit on the grounds of sexual harassment. She had been joined by a growing number of faculty who felt that, because the corridor in which the photos were hung was the only access to their offices and classrooms, the photos created a hostile work environment for themselves and their students. The provost wanted advice on what should be done.

Arriving at the art building to view the show, I found that the forty or so photos were hung, not in the art gallery on the first floor, but close together on both sides of a long narrow corridor leading to classrooms. They depicted close-ups of nude female bodies and female body parts, always with spread legs. Walking through the narrow corridor, there was no way to avoid looking at the photos. I personally found them grotesque.

When the curator of the exhibit refused to remove the photos or hang them elsewhere, controversy flared. At a faculty meeting concerning the exhibit, those who wanted it removed argued that the photos constituted a physical assault on women. They referred to the irreversible trauma to impressionable students that such sexist photos would engender. The obvious excesses of this position were matched by those who wanted to retain the exhibit in its present location. The latter accused their colleagues of an attempt to stifle all creative thought and art. A professor of English stood up and declared, "If we allow this kind of censorship of art, soon none of us will be allowed to teach the greatest novels and poetry ever written." Not surprisingly in such rancorous circumstances, no agreement was reached.

I suggested to the provost that the photos should be rehung in the art gallery, where students and faculty could view them if they chose to do so, but where they were not forced to look at them in pursuing their daily routines. When the gallery director rejected this suggestion, the provost implemented his own idea of a compromise. During weekdays when students, faculty, and staff used the corridor for class or work, the exhibit was taken down. But on weekends it was rehung, and for two days each week the corridor of the art building functioned as a gallery rather than a place of work. This awkward arrangement did not satisfy anyone.

I wanted to try to turn this dispute in a positive direction by organizing a serious campus discussion of the relationship of free speech, sexuality, and artistic expression. But in this I failed miserably. My idea for a teach-in was rejected by everyone involved, dismissed as an attempt to change the subject. As one faculty member cuttingly told me, "You're either for removing the exhibit or you're not—there's really nothing to discuss." Instead of an educational forum, accusations flew.

As it happened, active participation in this particular controversy was largely limited to faculty and staff. But there were, among the few students who became involved, several who had been part of my classroom debate on pornography. I was disappointed that although in class they had thoughtfully engaged these issues, in discussing the exhibit they resorted to a knee-jerk antipornography position. I could hardly believe the change in the tone and substance of their arguments. When I talked with them, they simply refused to consider alternative points of view to what they thought was the feminist position—removing the show. Was it possible, I wondered, that they had been totally unaffected by what went on in my class? I pressed them for an explanation. They defended themselves by referring to the large number of people on campus who were critical of feminists for even raising the issue of sexual harassment. With so many attacks on feminism, they said, they felt they should ignore their own doubts and support what they believed to be the feminist point of view. "You know how you can criticize your own family and see their faults, but when anyone else does it you deny it completely?" asked Frieda. "Well, it's the same with feminism. I might have personal reservations about closing down the exhibit, but I wouldn't want anyone to know it, especially if they aren't feminists."

In short, my students thought that to be good feminists they publicly had to be uncritical loyalists. What they were doing was adopting a position based on their assessment of their audience. If their listeners could be counted on to be feminists, they would say what they really thought; if not, they would adhere to what they thought was the party line. The problem of course was that this put both their personal honesty and intellectual integrity at risk. More, their inconsistency sometimes achieved a goal precisely the opposite of what had motivated it. Their disingenuous invocation of orthodoxy was all too often transparent. It not only made both them and feminism look bad but, ironically, often proved unconvincing to skeptics.

I watched with concern as this pattern again revealed itself several months later when Nadine Strossen, the president of the American Civil Liberties Union, came to Colgate at the invitation of the women's studies program. I had asked Strossen to talk about her new book, *Defending Pornography*, which she describes as a "women's rights–centered rationale for defending pornography."[2] In a packed lecture at the center, Strossen offered a spirited defense of the view that censoring pornography is harmful to women because it undermines their equality. She expressed her own personal aversion to pornography, but, as she did in her book, she vigorously criticized "procensorship" feminists. "I share [their] fears, frustrations, and fury," she wrote of feminists who would ban pornography, but "censoring pornography would not reduce misogynistic violence or discrimination . . . it would likely aggravate those grave problems."

To me, Strossen personified the model of a strong feminist, brave enough to be publicly critical of aspects of feminism that she questioned. I had hoped that the opportunity to meet and talk with her might encourage my students to be more consistent concerning what they believed privately and what they said publicly. But I had underestimated the depths of their resistance. In fact, many students reacted with fury to both Strossen and her lecture. They saw her as a traitor to feminism.

Immediately after the lecture a small group of students approached me. Two of them, Ami and Susan, were women's studies majors who had taken my courses, debates and all. In class, neither of these students had taken a procensorship position concerning pornography. But now they refused to concede to Strossen the right to oppose censorship publicly. "Why is she wasting a chance to tell the hundreds of people at her lectures about how porn degrades women? She is hurting the movement by attacking other feminists and by making pornography acceptable," asserted Ami. When I replied that feminists like Strossen showed courage in stating honestly what they thought, the students would have none of it. Susan, red-faced, finally blurted

2. Nadine Strossen, *Defending Pornography: Free Speech, Sex, and the Fight for Women's Rights* (New York: Scribner, 1995), 15.

out: "To me it sounds like she's in favor of pornography. She's not against it at all. I don't see how she can call herself a feminist!"

I was amazed to hear these students so easily dismiss Strossen's presentation. In her lecture, she had been very careful to discuss not only her abhorrence of pornography, but also her personal commitment to women's equality. She explained at some length the important role she believed free speech played in women's struggle for equity. It was obvious, however, that because my students believed her failure to advocate censoring pornography was antifeminist, everything else she said was rendered suspect. To them, feminist solidarity required publicly stifling the real disagreements that existed within the movement. An uncompromising antipathy to pornography was seen as the only acceptable public stance.

The question of pornography caused difficulty in yet another context, when a group of the center's student assistants decided to publish a gender-related literary magazine, *Allegorical Athena.* This project was conceived as an outlet for Colgate students' poems, essays, and artwork. I worked closely with the editorial staff, encouraging them to be clear about the message they wanted the magazine to carry to its readers. They did a terrific job of compiling written material for the magazine. It included work by both female and male students on femininity, masculinity, relationships, socialization, and the politics of gender.

Finding themselves short of student artwork, however, the editors turned to illustrations from books and magazines. When we met to lay out the material, I discovered that more than a third of the reproduced art depicted nude women. As art editor, the responsibility for these selections was primarily Ami's. Weeks earlier, Ami had been one of the students who had been so critical of Strossen's lecture. My first question to Ami was why she had chosen so many photos of nude women. I thought this choice was inconsistent with, even contradictory to, the message of the magazine. I also asked why she had selected two of the pictures in particular, for it seemed more than likely that they would be seen as pornographic by many readers. How had she overlooked that, especially in light of her strong feelings about pornography? I explained that I was not advocating censoring the photos, but I wanted to understand her curious editorial decisions.

The students at the meeting were visibly stunned by my comments, and Ami most of all. She denied that there were too many pictures of nude women. Instead she defended the importance of showing female nudes. "You don't understand. It's not like in the media where women's bodies are exploited" she said. "We want to use pictures of the female body because it is beautiful. We are celebrating it. It's not pornography. It empowers women by accepting their bodies."

What Ami and the others believed was that because the pictures were printed in a feminist magazine, they could not possibly be pornographic. Tammy, the managing editor, stuck to her belief that pornography was not present in *Allegorical Athena:* "I would know it if something was pornographic; and this isn't." In the students' view, it was legitimate for feminists to concentrate on the nude female body. When nonfeminists published pictures of nude women, however, it was a different story. Women were harmed. I replied that it made no sense to me that knowledge of the artist's feminist credentials was sufficient to determine whether a representation was pornographic.

As the conversation continued, however, a number of the students became alarmed that regardless of their intentions the publication of some of the pictures might indeed be degrading to women. In addition, I was able to convince Ami and a few others that the emphasis on the diverse roles for women and men that was communicated in the magazine's written selections would be inconsistent with an excessive concentration on female bodies. "I guess we should either have a bunch of male nudes too, or else show pictures of both sexes in lots of different roles," she admitted.

Voting to take the latter route, the students removed some of the photos they had previously selected and added new ones. *Allegorical Athena* came out two weeks later, and the students who had worked so hard on it basked in the glow of the many compliments it received. But Tammy's statement about knowing what was and what was not pornography continued to bother Ami. Later that week when I saw her, she referred to the fact that Strossen had quoted a procensorship Supreme Court justice in a similar vein. "He thought he knew porn when he saw it, too," Ami recalled. "I didn't really realize what Strossen was saying when she talked about the dangers of censorship. But I guess what she meant was that if there were laws against pornography, someone—maybe that judge—might even try to use them to ban our magazine!"

When my classes turned to assessing electoral politics as a strategy for feminist change, students were all but unanimous in support of efforts to elect more women to public office. They pointed with satisfaction to the increasing numbers of women in local, state, and national offices. These victories they considered good for women and good for feminism. Betty, a sophomore who told the class that her mother had been elected to her town council, was particularly enthusiastic. "My mom was a role model for all my friends. If girls see women running for office and winning—especially in state legislatures or in Congress—they are going to feel like they can do that, too. That's how they learn that women are respected and can do anything." Betty described how she and her friends acquired skills and experience working on her mother's campaign. "We never would have gotten so involved if it hadn't been a woman who was running. You can see yourself like them. It's great when women support women."

In the same class, Sarya argued that with more women in office, feminist legislation would be introduced and successfully passed. She and others cited class readings outlining recent congressional passage of laws affecting the education of girls, violence against women, and women's health care. Although there was no clear evidence linking the two, my students were convinced that these advances directly resulted from the expanded role of women in electoral politics.

In light of this strong consensus, there was always visible surprise when I told my classes that I disagreed with the women's movement's focus on electing women to office. In explanation, I offered a distinc-tion I consider fundamental: the difference between a strategy that works exclusively to elect women to office, and one that attempts to place in office women or men on the basis of the policies they advocate. In preferring the latter, I have taken a position different from that of many feminists. Contrary to the belief that women should always be supported when running for office, I believe that we should assess candidates' political positions rather than their sex. An identity politics asserting that all women are liberal and supportive of their sisters is naive.

Most of my students disagreed with me, clinging to the idea that women always can best be represented by other women. They were not persuaded when I pointed out that many women and women's organizations have been the implacable foes of the very positions the students themselves support. They know that already, they said, having read about Phyllis Schafly's successful defeat of the ERA, and they are aware that many women have fought to reverse the right to an abortion. Even when I point out that the Christian Right and other conservatives have run women for office, counting on women voters not to make the effort to look beyond the sex of a candidate, they do not budge. To many of my students, the belief that women elected to office will always support other women seems the very essence of feminism. Data I present that demonstrate the far greater divergence among women's attitudes than between those of men and women on such issues as reproductive choice and the ERA also have no effect. As one exasperated student finally blurted out, "How can you trust a man to support your interests? The bottom line is that women need other women to defend them. It's our turn now!"

It is the "our" that is the problem. My difference with my students and many other feminists is captured right there. In my view, feminism should not be primarily about getting more for women as a group. Instead it should be about creating a fairer and more just society. To vote for a woman who opposes reproductive freedom, who thinks women are to blame for the violence perpetrated against them, or who wants to force women out of jobs so men can return to their rightful role as family head, fails not only to promote justice, but also to advance the version of a feminist agenda I support.

While a wide consensus exists among my students that women rather than men should be supported as political candidates, they do disagree with one another when it comes to deciding whether feminists should participate in electoral politics at all. There are always some who are skeptical about electoral participation, though most students do favor such involvement. Usually two or three in each class have even toyed with the idea of running for office themselves. Kiyana was one of those with actual electoral experience. A joint women's studies and political science major, she had run for (and lost) an election for her school district, but she was enthusiastic about trying again in the future. "I really want to change things for women in this country, and I think that getting elected to office is the best way. No matter where you are, there are offices that you can run for and make a difference as a feminist," she repeatedly urged.

Though the electoral skeptics in that particular class were outnumbered, they were nonetheless outspoken. Belinda, for example, referred to how corrupt and corrupting "the system" was. She challenged Kiyana, claiming that the latter would have to give up her feminism in order to win an election. "It might be okay for you, but I couldn't compromise my principles like that," explained Belinda. "I think that feminists have to work outside the system where we can be free to say what we really think and push for the changes we believe in. Elections are too much about money, too corrupt, and too male dominated to ever really let a feminist in there." Kiyana stood her ground, however, arguing that compromises were necessary in whatever path one chose, and that at least in politics she would have the chance to directly affect people's lives. Most students supported Kiyana and were eager to vote for women candidates.

I understood why identity politics was so attractive to my students. It is comforting to have a strong group identity and to believe that women are mutually supportive and in solidarity with one another. It makes you feel secure, as if you belong. Especially for women, identity politics is also hard to resist because so often in the past women were told that they should refrain from pressing for their own needs in the name of some larger or more important cause. Over and over again, this argument has been used to deflect the struggle for women's rights.[3] The bankruptcy of deferring their interests still resonates and makes the identity politics of sisterhood, for many women, the only real feminism.

3. Barbara Sinclair, *Women's Movement: Political, Socioeconomic, and Psychological Issues* (New York: Simon and Schuster, 1996); Echols, *Daring to Be Bad*; Ruth Rosen, *The World Split Open: How the Modern Women's Movement Changed America* (New York: Viking, 2000).

My students' visceral reaction in support of electing women to political office is a part of that. The assumption that someone of your own sex thinks and acts as you do, understands and stands for the same things you do, seems obvious to many of them. The "difference argument," that women are different from men and similar to one another, is everywhere. The result of all of this is that I have found it a difficult struggle to be taken seriously when I argue with my students or with other feminists for a feminism of inclusion, dedicated less to promoting women as an identity group than to advancing the commitment to social justice for everyone.

The same issue arises in women's studies when I try to balance the pressure to treat the study of women as an end in itself, and my own predilection to understand women in a broader social context. In seeking a balance, I often am accused of not caring enough about women. Some are even skeptical about whether I should be thought of as a feminist at all. At best I am told that I am confused—that I have my priorities wrong. They tell me that first we need to take care of women, and then later we can have the luxury of worrying about others. I tell them we fight for justice for everyone, together, or we will never make a real difference at all.

For the topic of the required senior seminar I taught each spring, I chose an exploration of aspects of the contemporary women's movement as an agent of social change. My intention was for the seminar's dozen or so seniors to apply feminist and sociological theory to an analysis of the movement and of the disparate feminist organizations it has spawned. But no matter my agenda for the semester, the students always managed to ensure that an additional issue wove its way into our discussions. They returned over and over again to a subject they could not seem to get enough of—what it meant to be a real feminist. Regardless of the issue at hand, they inevitably tried to turn the conversation to their preoccupying search for feminism's defining characteristics and for the personal indicators that would separate genuine feminists from others.

For most Colgate women's studies majors the content of feminism is centered on choice. They often say that an ideal feminist society would be one that allows each woman the right to choose for herself the life she wishes to live. Students envision this as the kind of society in which they themselves could flourish. But problems emerge when they are asked to apply the principle of free choice to others. For despite their ostensible commitment to tolerance, my students tend to be extraordinarily judgmental. They do not hesitate to express their strong disapproval of many of the choices women make, and they are especially critical of other Colgate students.

Dana's comments during seminar one day were typical: "It's all very well to say that women should be free to be anything they want to be. And I believe it! But what about a woman who worries constantly about losing weight, or spends half her life in front of a mirror putting on make-up and trying to look like a *Cosmo* model, or who wears three-inch heels that will probably cripple her by the time she is thirty? I can't consider someone like that a feminist. I am all for choice, but someone who does that kind of stuff is just brainwashed by the media. She's not really choosing."

In the same seminar later that semester, Coleen made a similar point, tying feminist authenticity not to looks, but to relationships: "The heart of feminism is independence—women being free to make their own decisions. But the only way women can do this is by being woman-identified—they can't let men or the media or their male bosses or professors make decisions for them. So if a woman lets some man influence her decisions," Coleen continued, "I think she has really given in to social pressure. She may not know it, but that's not really feminist at all."

By emphasizing what they see as the antifeminist implications of the decisions the vast majority of women make in their personal lives, my students place themselves on the horns of a dilemma. They feel that their anger at those women is justified. But they are at the same time troubled, for their condemnation stands in contradiction to the feminist solidarity with their sisters to which they aspire. Furthermore, the vehemence of their attack does not fit well with their own verbalized commitment to free choice of lifestyle. The tension between these two poles—their belief in the validity and importance of women's ability to make individual choices and their harsh dismissal of the actual choices so many other women make—is confusing and painful for my students. It preoccupies their thinking about feminist issues, and thus is a subject that frequently intrudes itself into their discussions.

In attempting to reconcile their contradictory impulses—one toward critical judgment and the other toward solidarity—my students often resort to academic theorizing that purports to explain how society manipulates women into making antifeminist choices. In relying on these theories, my students believe that they have successfully avoided being unsisterly. Their forceful criticisms of other women's behavior, they maintain, are not directed toward women at all. Rather they strike at the patriarchy that they believe to be responsible for what most women do.

Inevitably, the media are identified as the worst culprits. Print media are consistently singled out for the most vehement attack. Students point to the girls and women they know—everyone from their little sisters to their mothers to their roommates—who spend countless hours poring over fashion magazines. It is their overwhelming identification with the supermodels so prominently featured in these magazines, students argue, that renders most women incapable of making choices for themselves. Instead, influenced by clever advertisements, popular stories, and the powerful pictures that surround them, women are convinced to buy, to become, and to do what they are told—to conform to someone else's image of what it means to be a woman. My students believe that, in this way, women are inoculated against choosing authentic feminist behavior.

I always allocate some time in the seminar for a serious discussion of these issues. I insist, however, that the students make arguments to defend their views, rather than merely asserting them. And I explain why I disagree. Their position is, I believe, deeply disrespectful of others, treating them as naive or infantile or simply too stupid to know their own real interests. What they are implying is that most women are both incapable of resisting social pressure and unable to influence or affect the world around them. I point out that by adopting this position, my students are, without any justification, making the assumption that they alone know how to choose authentically.

In our discussions, I make explicit the unflattering view of women embedded in their position. The portrait they paint accepts the most sexist of stereotypes—stereotypes they would normally reject out of hand: that women are weak, passive, irresponsible, suggestible, and almost totally manipulable. "Do you really believe," I ask them, "that women—well-educated college graduates like yourselves for example—are so mindless and gullible that they buy perfume simply because some perfume manufacturer tells them, however cleverly, to do so?"

Their response is always the same. They insist that their portrait is accurate: that society's socialization is so powerful that it is impossible for women to resist. As evidence, they angrily detail, citing commercial after commercial, advertising campaign after advertising campaign, that they believe to be responsible for women's obsession with their looks, their weight, their men. "It's so obvious," concluded Pam one day. "It's just impossible to fight the barrage of TV, music, magazines, parents, boyfriends, and everyone else telling girls to be skinny, blonde, and sexy. No one could withstand all of that." When, each time, I wait for their anger to subside and then ask, "But you do, don't you? Why not others?" they squirm uncomfortably, but remain reluctant to reconsider their point of view.

It is difficult for them to take seriously the idea that their peers might be as capable of, for example, resisting advertisements for eye shadow as they are, but simply do not choose to. Maybe, I suggest, just maybe, they buy it because they really want to. Perhaps they are acting as freely as you are. Pressing this issue in this way always leaves my women's studies students in a quandary. If so many women are actually choosing allegedly nonfeminist personal identities rather than being coerced into them, then it is possible that there is something more attractive about those choices than my students would like to concede. My argument also raises questions about feminist authenticity. If women are independently and freely choosing so many different lifestyles and identities, my students' implicit fear is that it will not be possible for them to decide which ones are truly feminist.

In fact, much of their intolerance of the insufficient feminism they attribute to other women seems to reflect my students' own insecurity about whether they themselves are really feminist enough. In criticizing others, they seem to be trying to shore up what they in fact are unsure of—the validity of their own feminism. Though they hate to admit it, many women's studies students are drawn to aspects of allegedly nonfeminist lifestyles. They care about their relationships with men; they worry about how they look—whether they are thin enough, tall enough, attractive enough; they, too, read fashion magazines and experiment with make-up. In all of this, they feel confused and guilty, afraid that they are being traitors to their feminist beliefs. The upshot is their continued effort to create a clear demarcation between what is feminist and what is not.

In this context, the issue that inevitably arises in class is whether feminists should, of all things, shave their legs. My students are deadly serious about this. Because it is so important to them, I have learned to control my strong urge to dismiss the subject as completely ridiculous. I refrain from blurting out: "Who could possibly care? What difference does it make to the world what anyone does or does not do with the hair on her legs?" But the fact is that my students do care—a great deal. Pat: "I know it seems silly, but if you shave your legs, aren't you just giving in to someone else's idea of what women's legs should look like?" As Pat continues, this time tortured over whether to use make-up or not, I realize once again that lying behind this seemingly silly preoccupation is an effort to grapple with what it means to be a feminist—to demonstrate her commitment. Revealingly she confides: "I don't want to compromise. I really care about feminism, but it's hard to know what to do."

For many of my students, issues of personal lifestyle are the essence of what it means to be feminist. As a result, the seminar often becomes a tug-of-war between them and me over their desire to focus on subjects of personal identity including clothing, hair length and style, personal relationships with men, musical tastes, and sexuality. I, however, refuse to allow the seminar on the women's movement to be reduced to a discussion of those issues. How could I let leg-shaving displace an exploration of strategy, women's rights, and social policy? My students, for their part, do not easily capitulate. So several times a semester—at the very least—I feel called on to repeat my mantra: "Women who are committed and working to end sexism come in all colors, ages, shapes, and sexual preferences. Their hair is short, long, permed, colored, or hardly ever combed. You just can't tell by looking at someone whether she is a 'real' feminist." My students roll their eyes, for they know what they will hear next. I will repeat yet again my insistence that feminism is about politics, about changing the society so that women are treated with respect and offered opportunities and the freedom to choose for themselves—not about skirt length.

I conclude each semester with student presentations of their senior theses. I require thesis topics to be confined to analyses of social problems such as domestic violence or economic discrimination, rather than allowing students to work on issues of psychological identity. Remarkably however, even in these reports, the dialogue has a tendency to drift to individual identity issues. No matter how often I bring the students back to the subject of their theses, no matter how often the question of defining feminism seems to have been talked through and resolved—sure enough, in the middle of the next class or the one after that, someone will raise the question of what constitutes a personally authentic feminism. Becky will mention with annoyance that there are so few Colgate students who care about feminism that the geology department has more women majors than does women's studies; Pam will worry out loud about whether she will be "compromising her feminism" if she wears a dress for the job interview she has next week; or Patti will criticize her roommates who, she says, think and talk of nothing other than the number of calories they have consumed and the clothes that no longer fit them. And off we go again, with the students leading the charge against those who are not acting feminist enough, and with me pulling them back to considerations of policy, tactics, politics, and social change.

Wendy Kaminer calls this tendency "therapeutic feminism" and argues that many young feminists, unable to distinguish between the personal and the political, equate "political commentary with the telling of a personal story."[4] Kaminer herself criticizes the attempt to make one's own life a symbol of political struggle, but she quotes Susan Reverby, a historian at Wellesley College, who remarks with resignation, "What do nineteen- and twenty-year-olds think about? They think about themselves." And of course she is right. Figuring out who they are is, in fact, a pressing and important task for young adults.

Although I understand the students' needs, I also know that social

4. Wendy Kaminer, *True Love Waits: Essays and Criticism* (Reading, Mass.: Addison Wesley Longman, 1997).

analysis is not the same as discussion of personal experience. In class, I insist that my students differentiate between the two and emphasize the analysis. Discussion of their individual choices, experiences, or identity can be linked to or even sometimes be the starting point for such analyses. Alone, however, a focus on the purely personal is neither rich nor intellectually challenging enough to justify its inclusion—except peripherally—in a college seminar.

In fact, I spend many hours with my students outside of class talking through their efforts to decide how they want to live and who they want to be. As I listen carefully, I often wonder whether there is not something more I could do to help them understand the narrowness of their preoccupation with themselves. I struggle to communicate what I found to be true when I was their age in the 1960s—that social engagement is a way to express yourself and your feminism, an avenue to discover and also to create who you are. I want to encourage them to think of politics—the struggle against injustice on a scale larger than in their personal lives alone—as an embodiment not only of their abstract beliefs but of their personal selves, too. But I often come up empty. "Yeah, Professor Mandle, but that was the sixties," they say.

Notwithstanding our differences, we do fine together. My seminar students are, most of the time, willing to indulge me. They put aside their personal preoccupation with whether they are good feminists long enough to analyze the problems women share in a sexist society. The unresolved, perhaps unresolvable, thread of worry about their own feminism remains. But as they develop the tools of social analysis that I insist they learn, I begin to see—emerging alongside these personal concerns and sometimes even crowding them out for a time—an intellectual involvement with, and an excitement and growing confidence about issues of women's politics and social change. Slowly, unevenly, they may come to believe that this, too, is an important part of their feminism.

Many students in my women's studies classes report feeling beleaguered at Colgate. They believe they are different from others on campus and think of themselves as vastly outnumbered. They are convinced that most Colgate students are hostile to women's studies, to feminism, and therefore to them. They share tales of being ridiculed for taking women's studies classes. One student in the introductory course reported that her roommate, in all seriousness, asked why she was "wasting time in that class, sitting in a circle with a bunch of other women, talking about your uteruses?" With experiences like these, women's studies students tend to develop a despairing view of what they describe as the "ultraconservatism" of their peers. Based on this, they typically believe there is nothing they can do to convince Colgate students to change their views.

My own sense is very different. Talking to students informally outside of class and watching so many of them respond positively to the presence of the center, I find they are far from ultraconservative. It is certainly true that they tend to dress conservatively and look conventional, pledge sororities and fraternities in alarming numbers, and only rarely engage in political discussion or progressive activism. Furthermore, there are occasional campus incidents of explicitly racist or sexist behavior. But notwithstanding the predominant stereotype of a typical Colgate student—cool and uncaring about anyone but herself, uninterested in politics or social problems—I find that both women and men undergraduates are an intriguing mix of confusion, ignorance, fear, and curiosity about subjects such as feminism. Despite my students' conviction that their peers are implacably closed-minded, my experience is that, after only a little coaxing away from their preconceived notions, most students are open to exploring and considering—even supporting—many feminist ideas.

As part of my introductory women's studies course, I often require the class to conduct an on-campus survey of attitudes towards these issues. They use questionnaires to collect information from equal numbers of Colgate women and men concerning their views on the women's movement and the changes it supports. Since respondents are not selected randomly and the students themselves are not trained researchers, the resulting data are not scientifically valid. Nevertheless, each semester the survey's respondents make up almost 15 percent of the student body, and since over the years the results have been remarkably consistent, the data are good enough to get a feel for what Colgate students think.

Working in small groups, my students compile, analyze, and report their findings to the class. Each semester the same reaction occurs. They can barely contain their shock. "I'd never have believed it if I hadn't actually done the survey myself," Linda conceded as she brought her report to a close. What Linda was reacting to in 1997 was typical of findings in other years as well—Colgate students are not overwhelmingly hostile to either the women's movement or the idea of women's equality. On the contrary, of the 368 students polled in that year, 329 checked off "strongly agree" or "agree" when asked if they supported the women's movement. Fewer than 30 agreed with the statement "the women's movement is no longer needed today." Not only did surveyed undergraduates overwhelmingly endorse the movement, they also supported the specific changes it advocates. For example, only 71 out of 357 students disagreed with the statement: "The changes made by the women's movement will make life better for men as well as women." Students were nearly unanimous in agreeing with equal pay for women, husbands' supporting their wives' careers in two-income families, and the sharing of child care between women and men.

Students in the introductory classes always admit that they do not know what to make of these responses. However, they are quick to point to two questions on the survey that seem to confirm their own skepticism that feminism is supported on campus. They show me that a majority of the respondents checked "no" when asked "Do you consider yourself a feminist?" Even more telling, according to my students, is the open-ended question asking for three words associated with the word *feminism*. The overwhelming majority of words listed are unmistakably hostile: dyke, bra-burning, extremist, man-hating, bitch, overbearing, militant, loud, ignorant, and femi-nazi.

When my students see these words on the questionnaires, they react strongly. Both in class and in their papers analyzing the survey, they return again and again to these disturbing responses. Though they were ready for antipathy towards the women's movement, they never seem fully prepared for the venom with which some of their fellow students characterize feminists and therefore, in their eyes, themselves. Katrina, a first-year student, wrote "I am really upset. I find it depressing, frightening, and disappointing that some people are so ignorant. It hurts me that someone would think those things of me."

Much of the animated class discussion provoked by the questionnaire centered on explaining the discrepancy between the generally positive reactions to feminist ideas evidenced in most of the survey, and the decidedly negative answers to the two questions concerned explicitly with feminism. Annie summed up the dilemma: "I find it confusing that people can agree with the ideals embodied in the movement and yet not consider themselves even remotely feminist." Reaction to this contradiction tended to polarize my classes, prompting arguments between the few students who read it as encouraging, and the majority who found in it more justification for their despair. In one class, for example, Sheila dismissed the negative responses to the open-ended question as unimportant. "I agree that it's disgusting, what they say. But there are so many ways they support the women's movement and the changes it wants. So what if they are hung up on the word *feminist?* Let's just drop it altogether." Helen had a slightly different take, but generally supported Sheila's position: "This really gives us a lot to work with on campus. I had no idea that most people—even the men—really like what the movement is doing. If we can get them to understand that that's what feminism is, we're home free." Anita also provided a hopeful interpretation. "I can understand where they are coming from. Before I took this class, I supported what the movement was for, but I would never have called myself a feminist."

The majority, however, were not so sanguine. Overwhelmingly the class believed that Sheila and Helen were naive. Priscilla was typical: "The other stuff is just lip service. Everyone knows it's cool to support equal pay and be against sexual harassment. That doesn't show anything. It's the direct questions about feminism that really count." Priscilla and others kept coming back to the open-ended question. They were especially angry about the frequent references to homosexuality. "It's amazing that the words *dyke* or *lesbian* come up so often," commented Enid. "I can't believe people are so stupid that they believe every feminist is a lesbian. But even worse is that they are so homophobic. They make it seem like being a lesbian is a crime—they use it to reject the movement." Cassie agreed, "I sure hope these attitudes are just at Colgate. There's no way to fight this."

In seeking an explanation for the responses to the open-ended question, students often blamed the media. In one class, Rachel expressed the anger, common among students, at the media's ability to manipulate opinion: "This just shows how successful and powerful the media and society are at filling people's heads with untruths. Where do you think people get these weird ideas about feminism anyhow?" Referring to the similarity in male and female responses, she continued, "Obviously the women at Colgate are almost as brainwashed as the men."

In all of this, my students rarely faulted feminism. They resisted my urging to examine the women's movement critically—to think about how its own shortcomings might have contributed to such widespread negative attitudes. Completely dismissing the fact that most respondents had indicated that they knew someone who was a feminist, my students believed that the only problem was one of ignorance. "They just don't have any idea what feminists are really like" opined LeeAnn. Even more important, the students in my classes remained pessimistic that they could do anything to overcome that ignorance. They felt overwhelmed by what they saw as the virtual omnipotence of the media and of feminism's organized enemies. In the end, they did not believe they could play a role in changing the negative attitudes about feminism.

In fact, whenever I raised the question of a solution to the problem of undergraduate hostility revealed by the open-ended questions, the only recommendation that emerged was a suggestion that the university require women's studies courses of every student. Francine's paper was typical in articulating that view: "Personally I think that the university should make every student take women's studies. That's the only way to counter the constant negative images of feminism in the press and in our sexist society. Then I think our results would be much different." But here, too, students left themselves out as possible agents of change. It was the "university" that should do this, not they themselves. Even when I pointed out the disdain that students, including themselves, have toward required courses, they were unable to come up with a better suggestion. Instead they settled for criticizing the media and despairing about the undergraduate population's attitudes.

What I found both remarkable and discouraging was that, even in light of the survey's ambiguous results, most students remained staunchly pessimistic about the possibility of change. Most flatly denied what to me seemed so obvious—that the presence of overwhelmingly positive attitudes towards feminist ideas could provide an opening to talk about and perhaps convince other undergraduates to adopt a more positive view of feminism. Instead, for them, the survey data confirmed what they expected to find: the task of making feminism acceptable was simply hopeless.

The Student Organizations

There were four different groups on campus dealing with issues of sex and sexuality. The most prominent of these was the student-run Sexual Crisis Resource Center (SCRC). It involved large numbers of students and administered a sexual abuse hot line, provided peer counselors, and offered sex education programs. Two other student groups specifically dealt with gay, lesbian, and bisexual concerns. The first, Advocates, was composed of both gay and straight students working to increase understanding of and tolerance for freedom of sexual choice. The other was the Lesbian, Gay, and Bisexual Alliance (LGBA), a support group for nonheterosexual students, to which only they belonged. The Sexual Issues Group (SIG), formed by the university administration during my second year at Colgate, also included students. Its purpose was to bring together students, faculty, and administrators on a monthly basis to "discuss and share" information about sexual issues at the school. SIG was established in response to an incident at Colgate in which the names of male students were written anonymously on the walls of women's bathrooms as a way of accusing them of being rapists.

The groups addressing student sexuality were an important part of campus life, and I wanted to encourage cooperation between them and the center. But I also wanted to be sure that neither the center nor women's studies was overly identified with the issue of sexuality. In insisting that sexuality be given a less than dominant place, however, I found myself embroiled in conflict. In different ways, students, faculty, and administrators all pressed me to place sexual issues at the top of the center's agenda.

In resisting, I emphasized the intellectual and educational objectives of women's studies. As an academic field it should not be responsible for campus counseling or advocacy on sexuality. Its was not primarily a therapeutic mission. Similar demands were not made on the departments of psychology or biology. I fought against the stereotype shared by many that women's studies—because it deals with women—could be reduced to a discourse on sexuality.

In addition, on a more pragmatic note it seemed wrong to assume that the women's studies faculty—simply because they were women or studied gender—should provide student counseling or support services. Without any training in this area, the counseling they might offer would be amateurish and probably of little value to the students. Furthermore, doing so would seriously interfere with their job of educating young people. I wanted the program and its center to concentrate on education, not counseling.

In the division of labor at universities, the area of student life is the responsibility of the administration. Nevertheless, through SIG it tried to shift some of the burden concerning issues of sexuality to the center. SIG itself had no budget or staff and as a consequence could be no more than a sounding board. It met once a month to talk about problems, conversations in which I participated. However, whenever its discussions led to the need for action or student education, SIG, and in particular the administrators who served on it, looked to women's studies. Each year the women's studies intern was beset by requests to implement SIG-initiated projects. The pressure became so great that I often had to intervene, informing SIG that women's studies would be willing to cooperate but would not allow itself to be made responsible for the sexual education or counseling of students. Neither the women's studies intern nor the center was to be used as an extension of the Office of Student Life.

It was not only administrators who acted as if issues of student sexuality should have a central place in the women's studies program. A number of its faculty members did, too. The issue of the sexual exploitation of women students emerged routinely at women's studies faculty meetings. Whenever it did, my concern was that it threatened to eclipse important business related to administering the program. The monthly meetings of the women's studies program's faculty had plenty to deal with in discussing courses, the center, and faculty scholarship. It was not, I thought, the appropriate place to resolve concerns about students' lives. My practice, therefore, was to prepare a detailed agenda for faculty meetings that minimized faculty concern with this issue and to try to adhere closely to it.

One fall, however, several women's studies faculty members asked me to schedule an agendaless meeting, "so we can just talk about anything we think is important." Even though I was worried about it, I felt compelled to consent to their request for this experiment, at least once. But just as I had feared, the meeting quickly became a highly charged discussion, not of the business of women's studies but of the "oppression" of female students at Colgate. There was an initial brief mention of pedagogy, but all talk of teaching soon disappeared as the subject turned to the faculty's concern about the student social scene. "I think we ought to be talking about what is without any question the worst oppression our students face—as victims of sexual exploitation," began Professor Koppleman. "Female students are raped and sexually abused all the time, right here at Colgate."

Others agreed, and Professor Koppleman went on to offer an example of what she called "Colgate's uncaring attitude toward sexual exploitation." She described a recent encounter with one of her students. "Fran came to see me last week and told me her best friend was raped when they were first-year students, but she was too scared to tell anyone about it. Her friend was so upset that she ended up dropping out of school. She stayed away from Colgate for a whole year before she was emotionally strong enough to come back and tell someone what happened." As soon as Professor Koppleman had finished, other faculty members joined in. Professor Nease generalized about women students as a whole: "This goes on all the time. Women students deal with the negative atmosphere by turning their brains off and just trying to fit in—conforming by allowing themselves to be used. They think they're having fun partying and drinking, but in fact they are constantly victimized." There was agreement that administrators routinely turned a blind eye to these recurring problems. Professor Stanton, who had taught at Colgate for more than a decade, seemed stunned by this information: "Is that still going on? I had no idea things hadn't improved for women students."

Expressions of anger and outrage were interrupted only when an administrator who attended women's studies meetings and who possessed extensive experience dealing with instances of student sexual assault on campus attempted to intervene. Barbara Lakey, the assistant dean of students, did not deny the seriousness of such a crime, but reported that the available data indicated that rape occurred on the campus much less frequently than the conversation was suggesting. She went on to outline the college's elaborate procedures for dealing with sexual assault, explaining however that if, as in the case described by Professor Koppleman, students refused to tell anyone or press charges, there was little the administration could do.

Dean Lakey's words fell on deaf ears. Some faculty, like Professor Koppleman, simply were not interested in what she had to say. Others became cowed after Professor McDonald snapped, "I think those kinds of excuses are unconscionable. We know what's going on here. This is not just about sexual assault, anyway. Women are sexually exploited by the whole social scene, especially by the fraternities, and you people don't do anything to stop it."

As they recounted students' tales of drunken parties and one-night stands, the faculty members worked themselves up to a collective fury. The objects of their outrage were male undergraduates and the administration. Women students escaped any mention except as victims. Faculty members seemed completely insensitive to the possibility that women students might be complicit in the social scene that was being condemned. To these faculty, women students were only exploited, used, and powerless. They were thought incapable of playing an active role in what went on, or of altering the situation in which they found themselves.

As the end of the meeting approached, it took an even more bizarre turn. Several faculty began to talk themselves into believing that they were the only ones who could protect women students. Most astonishing of all, their vehicle in this was to be women's studies. "We really need the center to speak up for women students and do something

about this," declared Professor Perotti. Faculty made several suggestions about exactly what women's studies could do. Professor Miles
said that Brown Bag lunches, instead of being oriented academically,
should be used "as a time when students informally could meet with
faculty and talk about the sexual problems they are having." Another
faculty member wanted the women's studies' intern to provide more
"counseling advice to students about their personal lives," while a third
suggested that we should organize meetings where women students,
with faculty help, could "get in touch with their anger."

My alarm at their assigning these responsibilities to women's studies
was eased only by the fact that, based on past experience, I did not
take their suggestions seriously. I had learned that no one would
take the time or make the effort to implement the plans they were
making. Nevertheless, what the meeting revealed about their attitudes
was disquieting. Their priorities were made clear by their eagerness
to deal with student social life while ignoring the pressing curricular
and academic issues in women's studies that needed to be addressed.
I myself had no objection to the expression of concern about nonacademic problems facing our students. But I felt they should be aired
in a broad faculty forum, not be viewed as the responsibility of the
women's studies program.

I also had serious reservations about the emotional tone of the
discussion that day. In order to be meaningful and helpful to students,
the understanding of and attention to their problems needed to be
considerably more sophisticated than what had occurred in the faculty
meeting. To grapple seriously with the issue of the sexual and social
life of college women required a great deal more than an emotional
catharsis based on what was at best questionable information. I would
have endorsed an effort by the Colgate faculty, not just women's
studies, to create a special university committee to gather information
about and analyze the lives of our students. But simply to assert that
the sexual exploitation of women students was all but ubiquitous, and
to resist attempts by others to provide serious information or analysis,
as the women's studies faculty had done, was more than inadequate.
It was irresponsible.

Most disturbing in all of this, however, were the proposed solutions. Not only did faculty members assume that they knew how

and why undergraduate women were sexually exploited at Colgate—they also offered up themselves and the women's studies program as undergraduate women's saviors and protectors. But if students were in fact in need of professional psychological counseling because they were being sexually abused, surely a group of professors of English literature and anthropology were not the people to provide it. If, on the other hand, female students were themselves choosing, as seemed likely from their behavior, to attend fraternity parties several nights a week, drink excessively, engage in multiple and short-lived sexual encounters, and neglect their studies, they clearly needed some help. But why would anyone think that these students would be interested in talking about these things with a group of faculty women who clearly disapproved? Women's studies was an academic program, not a counseling service. Furthermore, it was implausible to assume that an end to problems as serious as those the faculty had described could be accomplished by simply encouraging students to "vent their feelings" with faculty as the audience.

Too many of the women's studies faculty seemed unable to see that this plan was a disaster. If implemented, it would at once compromise women's studies' academic programming, place responsibilities on the faculty that they could not fulfill, and harm students by offering them a bogus solution to the problems they were experiencing. It was empty rhetoric. Faculty, untrained and lacking any expertise in this area, were in fact incapable of devising or implementing solutions to these problems.

But the problems were nevertheless real. As a result, it was not just the faculty and the administration but students, too, who often demanded that women's studies do something. Repeatedly citing "the incredibly dysfunctional relationships among women and men on this campus," they turned to the center for support. However, in contrast to the faculty's emphasis on the sexual victimization of women under-graduates, the students were likely to indict women's behavior as well as men's. "The social scene here is a mess," commented Sheila, as she and two of her friends sat in my office one day. "On a typical night, everyone is at the bars in town or at fraternity parties, getting drunk and then finding someone. No one talks to each other. People who had sex one night don't even say hello to each other the next day. They act as if they never saw each other before! A dinner date where you might actually have a real conversation with a guy is uncool. The only guys you can really ever talk to are your 'guy' friends." "Yeah," chimed in Ingrid, "would you believe a real relationship is talked down? A guy who has a steady girlfriend—a good relationship I mean—gets called 'gay' by his friends? My guy friends think this whole situation stinks, too, but it just goes on and on." Thus on the one hand, female students had no emotional connection with their sexual partners; on the other hand, they had no sexual relations with those men, their "guy" friends, to whom they were emotionally close. The irony of this situation was not lost on the students. "How do we ever put these two together?" concluded Ingrid with a sigh.

Perhaps in response to this situation, the center's student assistants frequently wanted to do projects designed to "build positive relationships." However, these were repeatedly the projects that students had most difficulty in successfully implementing. For example, one year Frieda and her closest friend, Maureen, were determined to organize a series of center-sponsored programs that they called "Relationship Education." Their idea was to go directly into the dorms, especially those where first- and second-year students lived. "We want to talk openly with younger students about our own bad experiences with alcohol, relationships, and sex at Colgate." When I suggested that they might be duplicating the efforts of First-Year Orientation and of the college's counseling center, as well as of the numerous publications distributed by the dean of students' office, Maureen disagreed. "No one ever listens to the deans when they give advice, but coming from other students it might make a difference. We want to approach it from the point of view of feminists, telling women they don't have to do this stuff. That's different! And anyhow it's worth a try."

I agreed, but knowing how attractive a focus on personal relationships like this would be to student assistants, I wanted to make sure that projects like this one did not dominate the center's work. I would only allow one such project a semester. That year, Frieda, Maureen, and I also agreed that their work on relationships would be only part of their overall responsibilities at the center. In addition, they agreed to include on the project only students not already working at the center; no other students assistants would be involved. Though they worked hard, in the end the project, like previous programs focused on personal relations, did not go well. It had difficulty attracting students to the dorm conversations, and when they did come they often didn't do much more than complain. Frieda was disgusted: "Everyone talks about how terrible relationships are around here, but no one really wants to talk seriously about why that is or how to change things."

Despite the poor track record of such projects, pressure was constant from student assistants to offer programs concerning personal issues and social relationships. Over the years several proposals to turn the center into a coffee house were floated, and one semester the student assistants became excited about their idea for a formal dinner dance sponsored by the center. Determined not to have the center turned into either a therapeutic facility or a social club, I vetoed many of these proposals, doing so most emphatically with regard to the dinner dance. I found that, with encouragement, students were usually able to then come up with projects on other issues they were interested in, unrelated to their own sex and personal lives.

Students not directly connected to women's studies also lobbied for a center focus on sexual issues. Among these, members of LBGA and the Advocates were the most persistent. Almost every year, conflict arose when they pressed hard for increased center programming on homosexuality and bisexuality. Our disagreement was not about the importance of such programming, but about its extent. Since the center's first year, I had turned over one or two of the popular Brown Bag luncheon slots to the Advocates. I also made sure that the center's schedule included academic speakers on these subjects. I offered both LBGA and Advocates the use of the center and assistance in doing their own outreach. What I refused, however, was to allow this issue—or any other—to dominate the center's agenda.

Lesbian, gay, and bisexual students, however, continued to demand more programs at the center, frequently accusing women's studies of neglecting gay issues. These students and their allies complained that women's studies programs only constituted tokenism. Because the center would not privilege homosexuality and bisexuality in its programming, they charged that it was complicit in the more general homophobia at Colgate.

The real problem was that the Advocates' efforts, including their ability to cooperate with others, were weak. The group was poorly organized. It was all the women's studies interns could do most years to coordinate with the Advocates on the Brown Bags dedicated to gay and lesbian issues. One intern exasperatedly told me: "I've spent more hours trying to work with them on this one Brown Bag than on putting together any other program all semester. These students just don't get it. They don't return my phone calls, they miss meetings, and they changed the date on me twice. I want to help, but this is really frustrating."

This was a recurrent pattern, so one year several lesbian faculty, staff, and I decided to call a meeting with LBGA and Advocates to encourage them to do more organizing. We told them we thought that they should sponsor more of their own programs. We also suggested that the ones they offered would be better received and attended if they did not continually focus only on their own personal stories, tales of how difficult it was not being straight at Colgate. We offered to help them figure out how to organize discussions that would educate students about gay rights. Our final advice was that they should work on coalition building with sympathetic student groups on campus.

The students, however, would have none of it. Lisa, the president of Advocates that year, defended her members: "You do not know how hard it is to be a lesbian at Colgate. It takes so much emotional and psychological energy just surviving, that we don't have anything left over." But Professor Turnbull, who had been in a similar situation herself as a lesbian undergraduate, would not tolerate such an excuse. "Sure, it's rough," she said, "but if it's going to get better, you have to do something beside talking about how bad it is. You need to get Advocates to do some creative programming, and stop just blaming everybody else." Her counsel was ignored. Instead the students turned to me, reiterating their demands for more center programming.

Later that spring, representatives of LBGA and the Advocates went to see the dean of students to request a center of their own. When she refused, they suggested to her that the Center for Women's Studies should partially function as a gay, lesbian, and bisexual support center, with the women's studies intern dividing her time between the two. I could hardly believe it when Dean Lisker called to ask me what I thought of this arrangement. My response was that under no circumstances would I shift the center's academic focus. I told Dean Lisker that I had no objection to the university's establishing a center to support gay, lesbian, and bisexual students, but it should be part of her office, not women's studies. When word of my refusal leaked out, I was labeled homophobic. Some LBGA members even insisted that my heterosexuality explained women's studies' alleged neglect of homosexuality and bisexuality.

My resistance to these students' attempt to alter the focus of both women's studies and the center, and my defense of women's studies' mission was, of course, not homophobic. It was consistent with everything I had said since the center was founded. I would not let myself be bullied by an accusation of homophobia into narrowing the center's agenda to issues of sexuality—of whatever kind. At root here, as in previous disputes with the faculty and SIG, was my belief in the importance of fighting the sexist idea that women, and therefore women's studies, should primarily be defined by sexuality.

In contrast to the demands by other groups dealing with sexual issues, the Sexual Crisis Resource Center tended to keep its distance from women's studies. Although occasionally we would join together in cosponsoring an event, generally SCRC student organizers worked by themselves. Their sexual crisis hot line and student education projects functioned autonomously. In fact, in some years, SCRC's standoffishness was so pronounced that it actually bordered on hostility to women's studies. Fluctuations in their attitude were linked to SCRC's continuing internal debate about whether or not the organization should be explicitly "feminist." Disagreements on this issue were never far from the surface. Some SCRC members vehemently rejected a feminist label, believing that it would taint their work. The other side argued that what SCRC did was feminist and should be acknowledged as such.

When the "antifeminist" faction was dominant, SCRC studiously avoided any contact with women's studies. In most years, however, relations between us were cordial. Especially when there was overlap in personnel between SCRC and women's studies—those years that many SCRC volunteers also majored in women's studies, worked at the center, or both—the friction and chance of misunderstanding between the two was minimal. For my part, while welcoming cooperation with SCRC, I was pleased that most of the time this student group worked on its own, running its hot line and educating students about safe sex. I respected SCRC's energy and initiative, and I hoped it would be a model for other student-run groups.

Two student-run events each spring highlighted sexual violence against women. Within a month of one another, SCRC sponsored a "Speak-Out on Sexual Violence," and the Women's Coalition, a group that during the rest of the year functioned as a feminist consciousness-raising group, ran its annual "Take Back the Night" (TBTN) march.

At the Speak-Out, selected students "testified" about sexual assaults they had experienced as children, as teenagers, or more recently as college students. In support, others read poems, recounted the experiences of friends who had been assaulted, or expressed their outrage at sexual violence. The event often extended late into the night, typically drawing a sympathetic audience of as many as two hundred students, faculty, and administrators.

There was clearly value to the Speak-Out. It was helpful to many students who had been victimized by sexual assault. The Speak-Out allowed them to publicly acknowledge the abuse they had suffered. Many students were helped by the deans and the psychologists from Colgate's counseling center standing by to talk with them after the event. To be part of the Speak-Out audience, listening to the litany of these young people's horrifying experiences at the hands of relatives, friends, and strangers, was powerful and moving.

And yet, for me, it was not enough. The Speak-Out audience was always drawn from a relatively narrow segment of the campus population—those who already were aware of and concerned with these problems. I could not help but feel that others, those who either ignored or were ignorant of the extent of this violence, should have been there, too. It was especially they who needed to be touched. And it would not have been difficult to reach them. SCRC could, for example, have changed the format of the Speak-Out. Microphones could be set up in heavily trafficked areas, and in that way expose much larger numbers of students and faculty to the facts of sexual abuse. But as it happened, other than putting up posters around the campus, SCRC failed to make much effort to ensure that its message reached beyond those who were already supportive.

I also had reservations about the content of the Speak-Out itself. Its format was limited to descriptions of specific atrocities experienced by Colgate students. No one explored the social causes of sexual violence, its extent, and how to prevent it or even lessen it. There was literally no discussion of what the audience could do to reduce the incidence of these tragedies. The goal of the Speak-Out was self-consciously therapeutic. It attempted exclusively to help those individuals already victimized. As one organizer put it, it was "a way to begin the healing process for individuals who have survived."

This emphasis on therapy and psychological healing was connected to SCRC's reluctance to be seen as feminist. They sought to avoid this label by excluding any analysis of sexual violence, and instead focused entirely on providing personal support for its victims. As one SCRC activist told me, "We don't want to frighten people away by raising subjects they might disagree about." They were not willing to venture beyond their emphasis on psychological healing.

When I raised questions about the limits of their approach to sexual violence, SCRC's organizers strongly defended it by arguing that the Speak-Out "empowered" women. I tried to explain why I thought that the kind of empowerment they had in mind was inadequate. I understood that participating in an event like the Speak-Out required great courage and determination, and in that sense assault victims were exercising power in testifying. Furthermore, talking about their experiences helped some students to feel psychologically stronger— also a kind of empowerment. That was all to the good. But the exercise of real power, I argued, would be to devise a strategy by which women could avoid or at least minimize the incidence of victimization in the first place. Ultimately a solution to this problem lay in the realm of social power, as opposed to personal or psychological power.

Over the years, I tried many times to convince SCRC activists that they should do more than apply psychological bandages to already traumatized victims. I also urged them to work with women's studies during the rest of the year to sponsor educational forums for both women and men. The Speak-Out, I suggested, could be the culmination of a series of campuswide educational programs about the causes, the laws concerning, and the prevention of sexual violence. We could take the message directly into dormitories, eating halls, sororities, and fraternities, presenting role-playing skits, lectures, and workshops.

My suggestions, however, fell on deaf ears. SCRC organizers continued to defend their original design. They maintained that the Speak-Out required so much time and energy that they could not take on anything more ambitious. But this was not the heart of the matter. For even when I offered to have the center carry most of the workload, they demurred. SCRC members were unshakable in their conviction that helping and counseling individual survivors was the most important response to violence. When I argued that without prevention and education there would be no end to the number of victims, one SCRC organizer answered: "I really can't understand how you can think about anything but giving the people who are already victims the personal help they need—right now. There are so many hurting people out there. SCRC has to support the people who have survived."

This disagreement eerily reflected conversations in which I had been involved almost thirty years earlier at the beginning of the women's movement. Then, as now, there had been contention between those feminists who emphasized the importance of individual psychological issues and those whose focus was on the need for political and structural change. In early 1967, when I first became active in the second wave of feminism, consciousness-raising (CR) groups were frequently the site of that conflict. As part of early CR groups, I remember the excitement we felt at discovering that much of what we had thought of as our own individual problems was actually part of a broad pattern of sexism that denigrated and discriminated against women. In these groups, we participated in the heady experience of recounting personal stories of sexism and receiving sympathy and support from other women.

But I, like many other early feminists, soon became dissatisfied with CR groups' continuing to function primarily as therapeutic support systems. We wanted to move on. The point was to do something about the problems that the CR groups had revealed. By analyzing sexism and then devising political tactics, we could act in response. But not everyone agreed. I recall speaking to CR groups all over Philadelphia in the early 1970s, trying to interest members in moving beyond personal discussions with one another to support a feminist political umbrella group for the city as a whole. I was truly dumbfounded at how few of the groups I spoke with were interested in making the leap from, as the slogan of the day had it, their "private troubles" to "public issues."

Feminists have always had to confront the painful choice of either servicing the otherwise unattended needs of women who are victims of sexism, or else working politically to end the sexist attitudes and behavior that produce so many victims.[1] There usually is not enough time or energy to do both at once. Something similar was taking place at Colgate. Student organizers of SCRC understandably had trouble resisting the immediacy of the unmet needs of their peers who were victimized by sexual assault. I empathized with those who, like the volunteers at SCRC, felt the pull of helping one person at a time—hands-on. But I believed that, especially at an educational institution, students and faculty had the opportunity to do something else as well. An organization like SCRC did not have to confine itself in the way that it did. Instead, if it had been willing to work with the center, SCRC could have balanced its providing individual help with education aimed at preventing the creation of future victims.

But as had often occurred in the early women's movement, the urge to help individual victims overwhelmed the need for political engagement. Despite my best efforts, I failed to move the students to an understanding of the importance of prevention. The Speak-Out continued each year, exclusively devoted to victims recounting their personal pain. My efforts to press SCRC did finally draw a reaction, however—a backlash against me. I was accused by some

---

1. In various forms, this tension has been replicated throughout the history of the second wave. Women organizing the early battered women's movement, for example, felt that they had to choose between helping desperately needy women with shelters and counseling, or lobbying for laws that recognized the full extent of male violence. The antirape movement faced similar dilemmas: whether to spend their limited time and resources setting up hot lines or escorting individual rape victims on the one hand, or organizing antirape marches and demonstrations on the other hand. See Susan Schechter, *Women and Male Violence: The Visions and the Struggles of the Battered Women's Movement* (Boston: South End Press, 1982); and Nancy A. Matthews, *Confronting Rape: The Feminist Anti-Rape Movement and the State* (New York: Routledge, 1994).

SCRC volunteers of being uncaring and callous toward victims of violence. Others thought that my suggestions were really attempts to destroy the Speak-Out. But for most SCRC students, not only I but the women's studies program as a whole were simply irrelevant. We had our priorities wrong. We wanted to analyze and educate while individuals continued to suffer.

Like the Speak-Out, the annual student-run Take Back the Night march also failed to raise the issue of sexual violence against women in a way that educated most of the campus. Each year, the Colgate march occurred on the same night as hundreds of other TBTN marches around the country. But at Colgate, TBTN attracted very few partici-pants. Typically, the march was composed of no more than a small band of twenty or so students and faculty marching from one campus building to the next.

A major problem in this regard was TBTN's policy of excluding men. The march's numbers were reduced because sympathetic men were prevented from participating. In addition, a significant number of female students and faculty avoided the march because of its women-only rule. Beyond this, TBTN suffered because in the past the marchers had on occasion been involved in unpleasant verbal confrontations as they passed by or chanted outside Colgate fraternity houses. These scenes, with fraternity members yelling and swearing at the marchers, were frightening, and there were some on campus who avoided the march as dangerous.

When I arrived at Colgate, TBTN was limping along. It was unable to attract more than a handful of participants, and its organizers were discouraged. Even they recognized that their march failed to do much to heighten awareness of violence or to make the night safer for women.

Two TBTN organizers, Lisle and Irene, were students in my intro-ductory women's studies class. Several weeks before the march was to take place, they raised the subject of TBTN during a class discussion of the development of strategy in social movements. Referring to course readings that examined separatism and the exclusion of men from the women's movement, Lisle declared: "I really don't see how the movement can be criticized for excluding men. That was an important strategy, necessary for women to build up a sense of sisterhood. That's why we made the same rule for the TBTN marches." After Lisle's comments, I decided to turn the class discussion to an assessment of separatism as a movement strategy. I announced that we would use TBTN as an example, and asked what role they thought excluding men would play in ending violence against women. As background, I briefly recounted the history of TBTN marches since they were first organized in the 1970s, and reported that throughout there had been disagreements concerning men's participation.

In discussion, the class was divided in their assessment of TBTN's exclusionary strategy. Irene joined Lisle's staunch defense of the policy: "This march is supposed to be about empowering women. That can't happen if men are there. It just doesn't have the same impact on the women. It's not about excluding anyone. It's a way of showing that women don't need to have a man to protect them to go out at night and be safe." Others disagreed. Karen, for example, countered that the reality was that—with the exception of a TBTN march—women in fact are not safe at night. "What good does it do to have one night a year when you're safe? What kind of power is that? The best strategy to end violence against women is to get as many people as possible to march in protest and to do it in front of as many others as possible. Men can and should be part of that. Especially since some men are the source of the problem, other men should be part of the solution."

Seleena tried to mediate. "What if they did what other schools do and have men march in the back of the line, or have their own march?" she offered. But the students opposed to including men would accept no compromise. Lisle said that it would undermine the whole idea of the march to have men participate because it was women who were supposed to be taking back the night. Jill supported her: "If we let men come, they wouldn't take it seriously anyhow. They'd ruin the march. And they wouldn't come in the first place unless they wanted to see what girls they could pick up."

This last argument was more than Karen could tolerate. "As feminists we're always objecting that we aren't respected by men and are treated like second-class citizens. And we're right about that. But when we exclude men, it's doing the same thing," she snapped. "It's really unfair to question the motives of men who want to support TBTN or to tell them to walk in the back of the line. To me, it would be great to see men—lots of men—stand up against violence. I know lots of guys on my floor who would come if we let them. To tell you the truth, we should insist that men come—this is their problem, too. And besides, that would probably shut up the fraternities."

The discussion went back and forth. It was clear that the two sides had different goals for the march. Those who wanted to exclude men were primarily focused on how the march would psychologically affect its participants. They made the assumption that the only way for the women involved to feel good—strong and empowered—was to be able to march together in the absence of men. In this way they would feel they were "taking back the night." For the others, the primary goal was to have an impact on as many people as possible. They wanted to reach people who were not actually marching but whose consciousness about sexual assault could be raised by seeing the march. The idea was to communicate a message, directed to anyone who would listen. The largest march possible—one which excluded no one—would best accomplish that goal.

At the end of the class when my students turned to me to ask what I thought, I told them that movements for social change constantly face choices like this one. What is required is that there be clarity about the purpose of the event. Deciding on a strategy involves answering the question of how a particular event fits into the movement's overall goal. I explained that I did not dismiss lightly the importance of feelings of psychological well-being and empowerment for participants. But, for me at least, this accomplishment was less important than actually making streets and nights and college campuses safer for women. That was best advanced, I thought, by raising awareness about the nature and extent of violence against women as widely as possible. While the exclusion of men might make some women feel good or more powerful, a woman-only TBTN march would have a negative effect on what I considered an even more fundamental movement goal: the creation of a nonsexist society. Women and men working together to defeat an aspect of sexism would be an important step in that direction. Finally, since a nonexclusionary march would likely be larger and better able to avoid verbal attacks from fraternities, it would probably attract more participants. Marchers in this way might come to see that real empowerment does not require the exclusion of male allies.

Soon after that class, posters appeared announcing TBTN, and to my surprise men were explicitly welcomed to the march. No one ever said whether the class discussion had played a role in encouraging Women's Coalition to rethink its strategy, but I like to think it had. What is more, the new policy was a success. The march was larger and received more attention than in the past. There were more men and women, students, faculty, and administrators than ever before, expressing their outrage at violence against women. The march proceeded without incident. Participants, including myself, found marching in TBTN an inspiring and moving personal experience. We could see that we were beginning to have an impact.

The Greek system at Colgate is all but hegemonic. Each year, over two-thirds of Colgate's sophomores pledge sororities or fraternities, and the social life of most undergraduates is dominated by fraternity events and parties. Nevertheless, two years before I came to Colgate, the faculty voted nearly unanimously to eliminate all fraternities and sororities on campus. What most bothered the faculty was the long association—at Colgate as elsewhere—between the Greek system and incidents of hazing, excessive drinking, sexual assault, and vandalism. Though the president and the board of trustees ultimately rejected the recommendation, the vote accurately reflected the faculty's hostility toward both sororities and fraternities.

Women's studies faculty were prominent in the fight to abolish the Greek system. Feminist literature is overwhelmingly critical of the sexism fostered by campus Greek culture.[2] The central focus of this critique are the misogynistic attitudes fostered in many fraternity houses. Colgate itself has had a number of incidents in which fraternities displayed misogyny. The most widely publicized occurred in the late 1980s when a document written by members of a fraternity was reproduced in the student newspaper. It was the secret record of

2. See, for example, Peggy Reeves Sanday, *Fraternity Gang Rape: Sex Brotherhood and Privilege on Campus* (New York: New York University Press, 1990).

fraternity brothers' written comments over a number of years in which they boasted about their hostility to, their humiliation of, and their sexual assaults on women. The fraternity was suspended for two years as a result of this incident, but reestablished itself after the suspension period terminated.

Sororities, too, come under critical scrutiny from feminists. They are accused of encouraging deferentially traditional attitudes in women. Singled out for special disdain are those sororities that urge their members to take the role of "little sisters" to male fraternity members, trading "service" to the men for their "protection."[3]

Ill will among the Colgate women's studies faculty toward the Greek system was intense. In conversation, one faculty member anguished over the subject: "I just can't understand why so many Colgate women have the bad judgment to be part of the Greek system." Several women's studies faculty felt so strongly that they refused to accept invitations to faculty/student get-togethers at sorority houses. Indeed, Professor Bartels, the chair of the Committee on Sexual Harassment, went so far as to decline to enter a sorority house when she was asked to lecture on, of all subjects, sexual harassment. She was totally unperturbed by my argument that she had been professionally negligent in making that decision. Her reply left no question about where she stood: "You have to draw the line somewhere. I will not compromise my principles by setting foot in any sorority or fraternity house."

There was a profound irony involved in the hostility to Greek-affiliated women on the part of feminist faculty. After all, sororities at Colgate actually represented the largest organized group of women on campus. As a result of the uncompromising opposition to the sorority membership that was so obviously important to their female students,

3. Linda Kalof and Timothy Cargill, "Fraternity and Sorority Membership and Gender Dominance Attitudes" (*Sex Roles* 25 [October 1991]: 417–23). Martin and Hummer summarize the empirical research on this subject and conclude that sororities as well as fraternities "promote a gender hierarchy on campus that fosters subordination and dependence in women, thus encouraging sexual exploitation and the belief that it is acceptable" (Patricia Yancey Martin and Robert A. Hummer, "Fraternities and Rape on Campus," *Gender and Society* 3, no. 4 [December 1989]: 468).

women's studies faculty often found themselves alienated from the very women to whom they claimed they wanted to relate.

Though I shared a deep suspicion of sororities, I made an explicit effort through women's studies and the center to reach out to sorority women. I was encouraged as I began to recognize that many students active at the center and enrolled in women's studies classes were actually members of sororities. I distinctly remember my initial confusion when one of the most articulate and explicitly feminist students in my introductory women's studies course turned out to be the president of her sorority. And indeed over the years, many of the most independent-minded and outspoken women in my classes were Greek-affiliated. My implicit assumption that there was a necessary contradiction between sorority membership and an interest in women's studies and feminism was obviously false. These women were not concerned only with parties and men. They filled important leadership roles on campus as athletic team captains, in student government, and as editors of college publications.

My curiosity piqued, I made it a practice to question my women's studies students about their Greek experience: why they had joined; what benefits did they derive from sorority life; and, most importantly, did they feel any conflict between their participation in women's studies and the Greek system? Their responses often surprised me. Some made sororities sound as if they were feminist organizations. To them, sororities were empowering for women. They helped develop leadership skills, encouraged women students to be independent, and reinforced their commitment to academic achievement. The idea of a contradiction between their affiliation and an interest in feminism or active participation in women's studies seemed incomprehensible to many of my students. Harriet, in fact, stressed their complementarity: "I really wasn't much interested in women's studies until I moved into my sorority house with so many other women. After living there for a year, I got to thinking I should know more about women's experiences and the way gender affects people."

Others, however, were more ambivalent. For them, the many positive features of their sorority membership coexisted uneasily with the sexism that they acknowledged was present in Greek life. They were troubled by the contradictions they encountered in their sororities. Suzanne was one sorority member who had thought a great deal about this. She noted with pride that sororities often talked about the importance of and encouraged high self-esteem in their members. But she also worried about whether this was more talk than reality. "If we're going to be really honest," she confided, "in sororities, self-esteem is dependent on what you look like, not on who you are." Suzanne was concerned that by stressing the importance of clothing, looks, and their bodies, sororities demeaned women and helped to raise their insecurity, not their self-esteem. Another illustration of a contradiction in Greek life was reported by Jill. She told me that while her sorority encouraged members to make independent decisions, it also undertook activities that she thought promoted women's subservience to men. "Sometimes I don't know what the message really is," she conceded.

As sorority women told me their stories, examples of these conflicts abounded. While they welcomed the social benefits resulting from their ties to fraternities, many sorority members resented the all-too-frequent humiliation they suffered at the hands of fraternity men. Sororities at Colgate boasted that their members had higher grades than non-Greek women. However, they actively promoted the partying and excessive drinking that tended to undermine academic work. Suzanne and others were upset that they were treated as "little girls" by their national organizations and not allowed to make decisions for themselves. But these same students often defended what they themselves admitted were silly and trivial sorority rituals. Many of those I talked to who were most ambivalent about their experiences in the Greek system nonetheless remained active members throughout their four years at Colgate. "All my friends are there," explained one. Others, however, disaffiliated as juniors or seniors. "I guess I just outgrew it," explained Rachael. "There came a time when I couldn't put up with the hypocrisy of saying you support other women and then talking behind their backs all the time."

Listening to them, I came to believe that women's studies might successfully offer students like these a way to intellectually frame issues of gender that could help them sort out the options and choices with which they were already grappling. First, however, I had to overcome the distrust that still existed for many of those on both sides of the divide between women's studies and the Greek system. Most sorority women, even those active in the center, still deeply resented the faculty's vote to eliminate fraternities and sororities. The prominence of women's studies professors in that fight did little to make either the program or its faculty attractive to these students. The continued hostility of many faculty toward Greek life was not lost on the students. One sorority member, Gerry, told me that she and other Greeks regularly refrained from wearing their sorority pins to class because they feared the faculty's opprobrium. Because of all of this, I knew it was important, right from the beginning, to make it very clear to Greek-affiliated women that they were welcome in the women's studies program.

My first intern played an essential role in this welcoming. As an undergraduate at Brown, Penny, in addition to her involvement in women's studies, had been a member of a coed fraternity. She passionately believed that these two spheres were not only compatible but complementary. Her presence at the center inserted a new tone in the relationship between sorority women and women's studies. From that first year on, I tried to build on commonalities existing between sororities and women's studies. One project drew on the sororities' regular involvement in charity work. During the spring of the center's first year, I approached several sororities with a proposal to link their community service with women's studies' emphasis on gender education and feminist politics. I ultimately secured the cosponsorship of three sororities for a joint effort to raise money for a local battered women's shelter.

In this joint project, instead of following the usual sorority pattern of only donating money, women's studies added an educational component. For example, when students raised money on campus for the shelter, they also gave out brochures and engaged donors in discussion about battering. In addition, student assistants at the center organized an evening program that sororities made mandatory for their members. The panel discussion featured staff members from the shelter, a woman who herself had been battered, and Colgate's director of campus safety. Each of the speakers explored the ways in which traditional gender stereotypes of masculinity and femininity contributed to battering. The campus safety officer brought the issue home to students when he recounted vivid examples of battering in student relationships at Colgate. In response to questions, he and the other panelists also detailed what women should do if they or someone they know are confronted with a battering situation. In the aftermath of this program, a number of Colgate students volunteered at the shelter.

The success of this event provided the foundation for continuing cooperation between sororities and the center. In fact, the involvement of sororities with women's studies was more extensive than I could possibly have anticipated. Over the years, Greek-affiliated women were among the most responsive to and active in women's studies. In 1996, for example, the presidents of half the sororities on campus majored or minored in women's studies, and the president of the Women's Panhellenic Council was not only a women's studies major but also actively involved at the center.

Some of these leaders began to undertake serious efforts to change sorority life at Colgate. One proposal made by a women's studies major, though unsuccessful, was to reform rush so that it focused less on the traditionally superficial meetings between sorority sisters and potential members. Ora explained, "I want my sorority to change rush so that how a rushee looks isn't what matters. We need to take the time to sit down and really talk about things to find out what kind of person she is."

Others tried to eliminate new-member induction rituals that were demeaning to women or where hazing had occurred. Cheryl was particularly dismayed at a ritual that routinely occurred at her sorority. In it, sorority members made critical comments about the bodies of new pledges, who were forced to stand naked in front of them. In some cases, this ritual included sisters' circling in magic marker those parts of new members' bodies they thought were too small or too large, parts "that needed work." Cheryl not only told me she thought that this was hazing, and therefore illegal, but also that it reinforced dangerous patterns she had learned about in a women's studies class: "There is too much emphasis on women's bodies and on being skinny anyhow. That's why girls get anorexic. We don't need to add to that stuff ourselves." Cheryl felt so strongly that when she could not get others to agree to the change, she disaffiliated from her sorority. She went on to write her senior thesis on college students' eating disorders.

The reformers were more successful at altering at least one aspect of the relationship between sororities and fraternities at Colgate. Colgate sororities broke away from the united governing council that brought them together with fraternities to decide Greek policy. Instead, the women formed their own independent council. According to Betty, a leader of the insurrection, she and many other sorority women rebelled against the fraternities' domination of the joint council because the men would neither listen to nor give sororities an equal role in decision making. Her justification was straightforward: "They just didn't give us enough respect." When I spoke about this with an organizer from the national office of one sorority, she told me with some awe in her voice that the Colgate women's ability to obtain independence from fraternities was unusual. "The Colgate sorority women really are strong," she commented. "They know how to run their own show."

Though amicable relations between women's studies and sororities became normal, I was nonetheless touched when in 1994 the Women's Panhellenic Council invited me to be the inaugural speaker for their Faculty Lectureship Series, explicitly requesting that I discuss the women's movement. I lectured on what I called "Three Myths of Feminism." Myth number one was that the contemporary women's movement had already succeeded in making women equal to men— that there was nothing left for young people to do. Myth two was the claim that the movement had and could accomplish nothing—that women were just as disadvantaged today as we had been thirty years ago. And myth three was that students lack the will or the desire to continue to fight for women's rights and equity—that they are too complacent, too selfish, or both. After I had finished my presentation and listened for almost an hour as students passionately debated where the women's movement was going and what it should do, I could not help thinking that I certainly had been right at least about myth three. It was clearly invalid; these students cared deeply.

The capstone of my work with sororities occurred in the fall of 1997 after three Panhellenic officers paid me a visit. The delegation explained that they wanted to include feminist consciousness-raising in their mandatory orientation for all new sorority members. They wanted me to lead a special version of the program that women's studies regularly offered at the beginning of the fall semester. The program, "The F Word," was intended to acquaint students with feminism generally and women's studies at Colgate. Some years it featured a panel of faculty, students, and administrators, each of whom offered a different view of feminism; sometimes, students met in small groups to come up with their own definitions of feminism and then shared them with the larger groups; other years, I used a short film exploring various definitions of feminism to stimulate discussion.

The "F Word" programs proved to be an excellent way to kick off the academic year. But I never dreamed that Colgate sororities would want to use the program to educate their own members. The sight of new sorority pledges trooping into the center—many for the first time—to participate in feminist consciousness-raising as part of their orientation to sorority life was astonishing. But the discussion following the "F Word" program at one new-member session was even more amazing. One of the students raised the question of whether sororities were or should be feminist organizations. With few exceptions, the recent pledges said little, but the juniors and seniors who had accompanied them to the orientation, two of whom were women's studies majors, made a strong case in the affirmative. Jenna summed it up: "Of course sororities are feminist. They are about women supporting other women to be the best we can be, to do anything we want to do. If that's not feminist, I don't know what is."

It is hard to be sure about the extent to which the center's policy of outreach contributed to the active feminism of so many sorority women at Colgate. Perhaps they were already predisposed in that direction, and the presence of a welcoming and inclusive women's studies program simply facilitated their expressing what they already believed. But I believe that their involvement with the program and the center played some role in developing their feminist consciousness. Over the years, many sorority women, including Jenna, told me as much. "I don't know what I would have done if it hadn't been for the center," Jenna offered as she said her good-byes the day after graduation. "I love my sorority and it really helped me grow, but women's studies gave me the knowledge and the courage to speak out against things that are wrong—even in Greek life."

It is not difficult to understand why the subject of abortion is a troublesome one for women's studies. Reproductive choice and especially abortion have, from the very beginning, been central to the struggle for women's rights. For most feminists like myself, a pro-choice position seems very much like the *sine qua non* of women's equality. Consequently for many women's studies faculty and students it is difficult—even in the name of good pedagogy—to treat antiabortion arguments in an intellectually serious way. They of course know that abortion is an extremely divisive issue, with people on both sides vehemently and emotionally tied to opposing points of view. But in practice, they are likely to assume, or to want to believe, that anyone interested in women's studies must be pro-choice. It is just easier to decide that, as one of my colleagues told me, "Since all my students are pro-choice, I don't see any reason to discuss an antiabortion position in class." It does take a special effort to teach about the abortion debate in a way that gives credibility to both sides.

I learned just how difficult it was when in 1995 a new student group, Respect Life (RL) formed on campus. Soon after, the center's policy of inclusion again came under attack by some of those most active in women's studies. The seeds of this conflict were sown the day three students representing the new organization came to see me. Chris was the group's spokesperson. "We're very interested in women's studies because RL really supports women," she declared. "Like Feminists for Life [a national organization], we believe that you can be a feminist but still oppose abortion." Explaining that she had been told that the center welcomed anyone concerned with issues of gender and women, Chris issued a challenge: "We want you to help us."

I was taken aback by their request. Though the center was committed to examining the many sides of feminist issues and had organized numerous programs exploring women's reproductive rights, it had never actually sponsored a program that took an antiabortion position. It was clear that women's studies and the center were identified with a pro-choice position. The campus group, Students for Choice, had been given a small work space at the center, and the women's studies intern frequently helped them with advice about organizing. I was of course aware that pro-life feminists existed, but it had not occurred to me to include groups like Feminists for Life (FFL) in the center's programming. After talking with these students, however, it was obvious that I would have to confront an issue I had not even realized I was avoiding. These antichoice Colgate students took themselves seriously as feminists, and they were asking that I include their point of view, as well as that of pro-choice feminists, in the center's dialogue.

Following the normal procedure I used when anyone came to the center with a project idea, I asked the RL students to write a proposal. In it, I instructed them, they should outline their organizational purpose and anticipated activities, as well as what they wanted from the center. I promised to give them a quick reply. Meanwhile, I contemplated the problem I was facing. It had two distinct dimensions. On the one hand, I had to make a decision about how to respond to RL when it submitted its proposal. On the other hand, I had to figure out how to deal with the negative reaction I knew would erupt from the women's studies faculty and its students if I said yes to RL.

The first problem was the easier. I was profoundly in disagreement with RL's point of view on reproductive rights; that was clear. To me, a woman's right to reproductive choice is at best incomplete and at worst meaningless without access to abortion. Furthermore, I have always believed that the essence of feminism is women's having choice in all dimensions of their lives, including reproduction. But at the same time I believed—equally strongly—that mine should not be the only point of view given expression within women's studies.

If RL could convince me that it was making a bona fide effort to address important issues of gender and women's lives—whatever its definition of feminism or its stand on abortion—I knew that I had to help them. There was no way that I could deny center resources to RL if they wanted to educate Colgate about women, feminism, or abortion. Despite my opposition to their ideas, I would have to offer them the same center support extended to other students initiating legitimate projects. Anything less would reveal as empty and hypocritical the program's policy of openness.

Once I decided that RL students would be making a claim on center resources I could not refuse, I turned my attention to the second problem—dealing with the reaction of women's studies faculty and students. This was much more complicated. There was no doubt that most of the women associated with the program felt so strongly about abortion that they would object to any relationship with, much less support for, RL. Anticipating a land mine when I announced my decision, I nonetheless called a women's studies faculty meeting to examine the issue and also arranged discussions with students working and volunteering at the center. In addition, I needed to find a way to publicly respond to the campuswide rumors I knew would soon be flying.

At the meeting of faculty, I summarized the content of the proposal RL had by that time submitted. I concluded by stating that, consistent with the program's policy of inclusiveness, I believed these students deserved access to center resources. Their goals were strictly educational and clearly related to issues of gender and women. I explained that RL had asked women's studies for meeting space at the center, cosponsorship of speakers, and a small amount of funding for posters and advertisements of lectures and discussions. RL had emphasized that their group was specific to Colgate and that it would receive no funding from anyone outside the university.

The range of opinions expressed in the ensuing discussion was quite wide. A few faculty immediately agreed with my recommendation. "We have to have a single standard that applies to all students, whether we like what they think or not," Professor Williamson pointed out. "This is a university. We shouldn't try to decide who can educate others. The center should be a place where everyone—whatever their politics or positions—can air their points of view, even Respect Life." Another faculty member who agreed with my decision was nonetheless concerned that inclusion of RL would weaken women's studies. She worried that pro-choice undergraduates might turn against a program that provided support to a pro-life group.

But these supporters of my position were a distinct minority. Most of the women's studies faculty vehemently opposed allowing RL access to the center. "These people aren't feminists! They're the ones who are bombing Planned Parenthood clinics and murdering doctors who perform abortions. Why should we help them do that?" argued a visibly outraged Professor Gereau. Others, more reasoned and less emotional, nonetheless maintained that RL's position on abortion placed it so far outside the usual feminist discourse that women's studies had no responsibility to include it.

The discussion was protracted, taking the better part of the afternoon. Even as it wound down, most faculty remained deeply troubled by the idea that antiabortion undergraduates would be any part of women's studies. But several, like Professor Schwartz, had reluctantly changed their minds, admitting that refusing RL was the lesser of two evils. "I hate to say this because I can't bear the thought of antiabortion women parading as feminists, but we shouldn't say no to RL. If we do, we'll just be driving them further into the antiabortion camp. You never know. Maybe when they're at the center, some real feminist ideas will rub off on them."

The very next day I met with student assistants and center volunteers. Like the faculty, most of them were furious that "their" center would include antiabortion activists. Lenna, the coordinator of Students for Choice, found it impossible to understand why I would even consider giving center access to people she consistently referred to as "enemies." "They don't belong here and I for one refuse to walk into the center if they are here. What would I say to them?" she asked. When I pointed out that she could engage them in conversation about what she and they agreed upon—that women should have legal equality and the right to equal pay and educational opportunity, she became even angrier. "Or better yet," I continued as she seethed, "you could take the opportunity to try to convince them that their position on abortion is wrong. If you really believe you are right, I think you should jump at the chance to talk to people who disagree." Lenna's face turned crimson. "I couldn't even look at them, never mind talk to them," she erupted and stalked out of the center.

There was silence after her departure as everyone stared at me. I swallowed hard and told them what they did not want to hear: that the center should not be considered "theirs." If it were, it would just become another homogeneous clique of students protecting their own space. I explained my view that including RL as part of the center's programming was a test, a very difficult one, of our commitment to an open and inclusive dialogue with others—especially those who disagreed. For the second time in as many days, I sat through a long and passionate debate about RL and about what women's studies should stand for. And again, when discussion ended, most of those present agreed to suspend their objections at least long enough to give coexisting with RL a try. But not everyone. Lenna, in particular, continued her adamant and vocal opposition to any accommodation with RL. A few days after the meeting, she and three other student assistants resigned from their positions at the center.

I had one more task to accomplish in dealing with the reaction to RL's inclusion. I needed to find a way to stanch Colgate's rumor mill. As in most small communities where rumors abound, I knew wild stories about women's studies would soon circulate. I could imagine irate phone calls denouncing the center for renouncing its feminist commitment or ones claiming that it was actively working to defeat *Roe v. Wade*. To fend off such rumors, I published a detailed explanation of the RL decision in the bimonthly *Women's Studies Newsletter*. In it, I spelled out my conviction that academic women's studies programs should encourage the full intellectual exploration of issues of gender and women. Despite my personal disagreement with much of what RL had to say, I made clear that they were welcomed along with everyone else to the center's continuing conversation. I ended the column with a quote from Anna Quindlen: "In the fight to keep women free it is important to remember this: freedom of speech is the bedrock of it all. Silence is what kept us in our place too long. If we now silence others, our liberty is false."[4]

My public statement not only worked to halt the rumors, it also produced more positive feedback than anything I had ever written for the newsletter. Several faculty stopped me on campus to tell me how much they respected women's studies' decision to include RL. A few students mentioned that though they themselves were not sure what their position on abortion was, the center's openness encouraged them to explore the issue further. One member of the faculty whom I did not know sent me a personal note that I found especially moving. "I have often felt uncomfortable about participating in women's studies,"

4. Anna Quindlen, *New York Times*, October 7, 1992, 23A.

Professor Kirchner wrote, "because, though I consider myself a feminist, as a Catholic I have some questions about abortion. I know we disagree, but I thank you for making it possible for me to contribute, in my own way, to a program I believe in."

Overall, the RL decision made clear to the campus, once and for all, women's studies' commitment to inclusiveness. Though RL's participation at the center did upset many campus feminists, only one or two were angry enough to permanently sever their relationship with the program. By the following year, even Lenna had reconsidered and was again involved at the center. She privately admitted to me that she had been "really immature last year," not sure enough of her own opinions to be willing to confront anyone who thought differently. "But now all that's changed," she added cheerily. The RL decision also attracted some new students and faculty to women's studies. Its full impact was symbolized by what one student wrote in applying for a student assistantship at the center: "I want you to know that I am a born-again Christian and do not believe that abortion is acceptable. But I just declared my women's studies major and I think the center is doing great work. It's where I want to be next year, working on a project raising the aspirations of local high school girls."

RL was short-lived at Colgate. When by mid-November the organization had still not attracted enough support to sustain it, the three original students abandoned their attempt to form a chapter. Before its demise, however, it did manage to sponsor one event, a lecture by a national officer of Feminists for Life. In light of the public nature of the RL controversy, it was no surprise that the FFL lecture caught the attention of many on campus, including women's studies students and faculty. At the center, an active debate raged concerning the appropriate response to the campus visit of a representative of FFL. Many of those most closely associated with women's studies advocated boycotting the lecture. "If we go, we are as much as saying that we support her point of view," stated Rebecca, as she and other students sat drinking coffee one day at the center. "Besides, as a women's studies major, I certainly don't want to hear her explain why she thinks abortion should be outlawed." But other students disagreed. "We're not going there to support her," countered Justine, "but why should we let her say anything she wants to without anyone disagreeing? We need to be there to challenge her when she makes things up. I don't want the audience to only hear her point of view."

The evening of the lecture, a large contingent of pro-choice students and faculty, including myself, was in the crowded audience. As I listened, I realized how ingenious the speaker's approach was, as she tried to link feminism with opposition to abortion. She employed feminist concerns with violence, rape, and equality in her argument. She was not afraid to use feminist rhetoric. She paraded her own participation in the civil rights and antiwar movements, as well as in the feminist struggle against wife battering and sexual assault. Her implacable opposition to abortion was consistent with these activities, she argued, because abortion was just another form of male violence against women. Abortion was antiwomen, occurring only as the result of men's coercing and manipulating women. She went so far as to claim that the procedure itself constituted a rape of the uterus. To fight abortion was to fight for equality and freedom because abortion destroyed the rights of the fetus. As feminists, she concluded, women must stand against rape, oppression, coercion, and therefore abortion.

When she finished, the audience sat stunned. After taking a few minutes to recover, however, many hands went up to object to her strategy of using feminism to attack choice. A heated discussion followed. I joined in the fray, criticizing as insulting to women the assumption that underlay FFL's entire position—their claim that women are unable to make their own decisions about obtaining an abortion. I accused the FFL speaker of infantalizing women. The discussion continued well into the evening and by the end there was no doubt that everyone— the speaker and her audience—had had a chance to fully express their views. This of course was precisely what I had hoped for when I agreed to RL's request that women's studies cosponsor the lecture.

I could not have been less prepared, therefore, when Chris and other RL students angrily arrived at my office early the next morning, accusing me of deception and women's studies of bad faith. "You said the center would support our programming if we tried to educate the campus," sputtered Chris. "But you undermined us. The women's studies people like you who came to the lecture didn't do anything but argue and try to show that we were wrong. That's just not fair!" I felt that I was experiencing déjà vu as I tried to explain to these students, as I had done months earlier to pro-choice advocates objecting to RL, that supporting a program did not necessarily imply agreement. I told them the center's goal was to encourage a dialogue that allowed everyone to articulate their points of view, and that I, like others, had the right to state mine. Unappeased, like Lenna before them, they told me that they were cutting off relations with the center and they refused to discuss further collaboration.

The Students

The 1995 anniversary of twenty-five years of coeducation at Colgate was the occasion for considerable soul-searching by the faculty and administration. The question of equity for women students in co-educational institutions was discussed both formally and informally throughout the year. These conversations revealed anxiety present among a number of faculty members that women students could not be well educated in a setting where men were present.

This point of view was dramatically articulated during an alumni reunion when a panel discussed the state of women's education at Colgate. Awaiting my turn to speak, I listened while two other faculty members offered their thoughts. The first, Professor Walls, had been a faculty member in 1970 when Colgate first decided to admit women. He described the college then and speculated on the administration's decision to enroll women. Professor Walls explained it primarily as a response to the shrinking pool of acceptable male applicants. The thought was that including women would expand the number of po-tential undergraduates who could meet Colgate's twin criteria of high academic standing and family income sufficient to pay the college's steep tuition. According to Professor Walls, the decision to go coed was decidedly not motivated by ideas of fairness or justice for women.

In fact, he reported, there were many objections voiced by both alumni and faculty to admitting women. Professor Walls had himself favored coeducation, and he was at the time widely criticized, even accused of being a traitor to "Colgate traditions." But to his surprise, within a year of the matriculation of the first class that included women, most objections to coeducation had evaporated. Not unimportant in this change of heart was what Professor Walls described as "good old-fashioned self-interest."

> Once the faculty saw how it was actually working, most of them concluded that women's admission was the best thing that ever happened to Colgate. Everyone recognized that it had significantly raised the level of intellectual discourse on campus. We had better students in our classes after 1970, and every faculty member liked that. As for the alumni, a whole lot of them dropped their opposition to women when they realized that their own daughters or nieces might be able to graduate from their alma mater.

Professor Ocha, the faculty member speaking next, pounced on Professor Walls's comments. "That's exactly the problem," she declared. "No one ever thought about what might be good for the women involved. They just figured they could get some better students and lots of tuition out of the bargain. Although I had not yet arrived on campus at the time, I believe that coeducation benefited Colgate but hurt the women who entered in those early classes." Professor Ocha then proceeded to share a number of horror stories she had been told by members of the first group of Colgate women students. When she finished recounting those tales, she declared, "The administration didn't understand and probably didn't care about real coeducation. They thought they could just add women and stir."

As she continued to criticize coeducation, what became clear was that Professor Ocha's assessment of the situation at Colgate was part of a more general disapproval. In fact, she believed that coeducation would always fail women students. It was her view that female and male students—both then and now—have "such different ways of learning" that most coeducational settings prevent women from flourishing academically. She affirmed the often-heard claim that coeducation inevitably constitutes a "chilly climate" for women.[1] By way of contrast, she spoke glowingly of her own personal experience as an undergraduate at a small all-women's college. The only way, she

1. Bernice Resnick Sandler, *The Classroom Climate: A Chilly One for Women?* (Washington, D.C.: National Association for Women in Education, 1982).

argued, that a coeducational setting could come close to that experience would be if it was willing to take into consideration what she called "women's special needs." But that kind of "real coeducation," she concluded, did not exist at Colgate.

Then it was my turn. I argued that whatever might have been the case twenty-five years ago when women first arrived at Colgate, Professor Ocha's negative portrait of Colgate today was a distortion. At Colgate there was evidence of women's accomplishment wherever you looked. Whether it was numbers admitted, grade point averages, student leadership, or the percentage of female undergraduates in many "male" disciplines, including chemistry and biology, women at Colgate did as well as or better than men. Furthermore, I pointed out, women, including well-known feminists, held many positions of authority and prestige both within the college faculty and the administration.

I did not claim that Colgate's implementation of educational equality between women and men was perfect. For example, despite progress since the passage of Title IX over two decades ago, Colgate, like most other colleges, still fell far short of providing equity to women in athletics. Even more importantly, the social atmosphere for students, dominated by fraternities, continued to be a serious problem. These and other areas required not only constant vigilance but significant change. But that did not lessen the fact that, in the classroom and with regard to faculty interaction with students, coeducation at Colgate was, in my opinion, not only "real," but by and large good for women students.

I noted that when Bernice Sandler coined the term "chilly climate," she had argued that it "focuses on subtle ways in which women are treated differently—ways that communicate to women that they are not quite first-class citizens in the academic community."[2] I reported that when Sandler had visited the campus two years earlier at the invitation of women's studies, she had been very impressed with the job the college was doing for women. After a day of meetings with faculty, administrators, and students, she concluded her public lecture

2. Bernice R. Sandler, *The Campus Climate Revisited: Chilly for Women Faculty, Administrators, and Graduate Students* (Washington, D.C.: Association of American Colleges, 1986), 1.

in the evening by saying that she had found no chilly climate. "I only wish all campuses I visit were as good for women as this one."

I ended my presentation to the alumni by answering Professor Ocha's brief for single-sex education. My argument was that coeducation benefits both women and men. It prepares both to interact and work with one another after they graduate. Women, I maintained, do not have special needs that require protection from competition with men. Indeed, the claim that they cannot keep up not only is false, but also serves to plant seeds of doubt in women's minds about their own abilities. When given the chance, as at Colgate, women have shown that they can compete effectively with men as well as with other women.

But doubts remained. Later that year I again encountered skepticism about coeducation, this time, remarkably, from the president of the college. As we chatted over lunch, President Jeffries mentioned that he had been thinking seriously about teaching a women-only math class. I knew that President Jeffries occasionally taught undergraduate math courses, but I had no idea that he or anyone else had been contemplating separating female and male undergraduates into different classes. He explained his idea, noting that in most math classes, women were significantly outnumbered by men. This imbalance created, he reasoned, so much discomfort that female undergraduates were discouraged from excelling in class. He was convinced of the merit of separate classes for women, he explained, when he remembered his own high school experience. "My parents made me transfer to a coed high school in tenth grade. It was terrible. In fact I was so miserable and intimidated that after a month I convinced them to let me go back to my old all-boys school." Jeffries thought that female undergraduates might be feeling the way he had at the coed school. He was sure that only in an all-female math class would he, as a professor, really be able to teach women and meet their special needs.

I knew that President Jeffries's proposal was well intentioned. He was trying to do something he thought would help women. He wanted to be sure that they received the best education possible and he was willing to go out of his way to ensure that. But his good intentions did not in the least lessen my antipathy to his suggestion. I thought that his idea for all-women math classes was deeply insulting to women undergraduates. He obviously believed that they were easily frightened by the presence of male students and just could not keep up. What was worse, his suggestion for separate classes, if carried out, would reinforce precisely what I believed had to be eliminated: traditional stereotypes that depicted women as fragile and in need of special teaching techniques, handling, and protection. I remonstrated at length with him. But when lunch ended I still had not been able to shake his conviction that female undergraduates needed special math classes, segregated by sex.

The president never did follow up on his idea to offer a women-only math course, but a third similar encounter occurred soon after my discussion with him. On the first day of the following semester I talked with a distressed women's studies faculty member, Professor Jordon. "I have a problem," she confided, "I just don't know what to do. I know that my women students are going to be too intimidated to say what they really think. There are four men in my women's studies class."

What Professor Jordon really was saying was that, like both Professor Ocha and President Jeffries, she believed coeducation necessarily impaired women's ability to learn. That was the only way she could have made the assumption that four men would silence the twenty-two women in her classroom. Without waiting to see if she was right, Professor Jordon had told her women students that they should not censor themselves just because there were men around, and had announced to the men that they should not expect to dominate the class. From the very first day of class, then, Professor Jordon had thought of students of both sexes as if they were cardboard stereotypes: the men domineering and always demanding the center of attention, and the women unable to stand up for themselves.

Troubled by these conversations, I decided to raise the subject of coeducation in my introductory women's studies course. I assigned the students a packet of readings representing opposing viewpoints on the question of single-sex education for girls. One side of the issue typically advocated either sex-segregated education or arrangements similar to President Jeffries's suggestion that female and male students within a coed environment should be separated for specific classes or tasks. The other side rejected the notion that girls were at a disadvantage in coeducational settings. It argued that sex-segregated arrangements deny girls equal educational opportunities and the chance to test themselves against a full range of competition. Advocates of coeducation also warned that the isolation of boys in all-male institutions tends to encourage misogynist attitudes in them.

My students had a deeply ambivalent reaction to this material. Despite the fact that they themselves had chosen to attend a coeducational institution, there was extensive sympathy for single-sex education. Many students argued that isolating girls from boys was especially necessary during junior high and high school years. Jayne, a bright and articulate sophomore, was typical: "I went to an all-girls school. I got a great education. I think it was very important for me to get the attention I got from the teachers without any boys around. Otherwise I think I wouldn't have been confident enough to compete and handle Colgate like I can now. I don't need that protection any more." Others agreed with Jayne that high school coeducation was devastating to girls, and they offered as evidence stories from their own schools. "I was good at math until tenth grade," recounted Dory. "Then I took calculus in a class with almost all boys. On the first day, the teacher said, 'Well, I see that we have some *real* math students here' and looked right at me as if to say that I wasn't one of them. That did it! Any math ability I had dissolved overnight. I suffered through every minute of that class."

But other students disagreed with Jayne and Dory's conclusion that sex-segregated education was better for girls. They countered that they themselves had done fine in coeducational schools, and they pointed out that Dory had ended up getting good enough grades to be admitted to Colgate. They also noted that the special attention and high-caliber education provided by all-girls schools might have more to do with the fact that most of them are expensive private schools with small classes than with the absence of boys. Nonetheless, the argument that girls are shortchanged by coeducation won the day in almost every class.

My students' ready acceptance of the necessity for girls to learn separately disappeared, however, when it came closer to home. When I described President Jeffries's suggestion of special all-women math classes at Colgate, they were unanimously outraged. "I wouldn't be caught dead in an all-women math class," blurted out Stephanie.

"There's no way that people would think it was anything but remedial. What does he think—that women can't do math? We don't need special classes. I had the highest math grades in my entire high school." Others echoed Stephanie's resentment at the idea that women students in Colgate classes should be treated in any way differently from men. Peggy then told her own horror story—about a high school teacher who thought women should be treated differently:

> It was my junior year. In physics one day, my teacher announced that every Wednesday would be, as he put it, "Ladies Day." That day only girls—there were seven of us—could talk in class. He said he wanted us to be comfortable, and he was worried that we wouldn't speak up any other way because there were so many boys in the class. But to me that was the worst! It meant he thought something was wrong with me because I was a girl—that I couldn't or shouldn't talk the other four days. So I didn't.

Peggy's teacher was obviously trying to be fair, but his preoccupation with the alleged differences between the sexes and his belief that girls would be so intimidated in coed science classes that they needed special attention had actually ended up destroying Peggy's interest in science. "I hated that class," she concluded. "I felt like some kind of freak. No more science classes for me after that!"

Though they did not seem to recognize it, many of my students were simultaneously on both sides of this issue. They strongly affirmed what they took to be the "feminist" opposition to coeducation, repeating its assertions that coeducation harms women and that women have the need for and right to separate educational institutions. The distinction they tried to draw between high school and college was not convincing, however, and when pressed they would repeatedly come down on the side of all-female institutions at every level of education. Yet at the same time, they supported the principle of educational equality, vigorously objecting to the exclusion of women from all-male learning environments. Furthermore, by their own admission, they themselves were doing well at a coeducational institution and they believed that they and other women were treated fairly. The contradiction between their harsh criticisms of coeducation and their actual choice of coed Colgate was, of course, striking. In the same breath that they voiced reservations about coeducation, they defended Colgate and defied anyone who would treat them educationally as second-class citizens. When I pointed to this contradiction, their typical response was "Colgate's different, you know. It's not like this at other places."

Faculty in the physical and biological sciences are typically underrepresented in or, more often, totally absent from women's studies programs. Issues of gender usually fall within the humanities or the social sciences. Science faculty are not trained to study the sources and impact of gender on human societies. There are exceptions of course, especially in a field like biology where the study of sex differences is part of the discipline. But in the sciences generally this is not the case. A physicist does not typically possess the expertise to study why there are so few women physicists. Questions of the role of gender in science or the position of women within the profession are more likely to be the object of inquiry by historians, philosophers, or sociologists.

The absence of scientists in women's studies programs creates a serious problem. Because of it, women's studies risks giving the impression that the sciences are irrelevant to or somehow exist outside the scope of issues of interest to women or feminists. That of course is not true. I wanted to find a way to include in women's studies serious engagement with relevant scientific issues, even though at Colgate, as elsewhere, few science faculty were involved in the program.

The harmful gap between science and women's studies was revealed by Anna, a sophomore who was in the throes of trying to decide on a major. Anna was a student in one of my women's studies classes and in the course of conversation one day she announced that she had "a real problem":

> Ever since I was a little girl I've wanted to be a research chemist. I still do. But now I am beginning to realize how important feminism is to me and I don't know what to do. Can I be a feminist and a scientist? I love chemistry, but I get so angry because I don't see any commitment to feminism and women's studies in the chemistry department. Over there it is as if women's studies doesn't even exist. I feel like a traitor to chemistry every time I walk into a women's studies class, and I feel like I have to hide my

passion for women's studies whenever I am around my science friends. I hate being split in two.

The day after our discussion, I called Professor Agee, a member of the biology department, who I knew to be an enthusiastic supporter of the program, to talk about the absence of science faculty in women's studies. I described Anna's dilemma to her. Professor Agee replied that she well understood Anna's predicament because she often felt torn in much the same way. "You know I'd love to teach in women's studies. But what course would I offer? My research on invertebrates doesn't exactly make me an authority on feminism. I'd be glad to give a talk on what it is like to be a woman biologist, but that's far from a whole course. Face it—addressing feminist issues as scholars is just not what most scientists can do." I knew she was right.

But something else Professor Agee said stuck with me. We were talking about why relatively few college women majored in the sciences. Almost in passing, she had commented, "I'm certainly not an expert on this subject, but it's something I think about a lot. I'll bet there are plenty of other science faculty who would really be interested in hearing someone discuss the lack of women in science." The more I thought about what she had said, the more convinced I became that, even in the absence of formal courses, it was important to try to use center programming to bridge the gap between women's studies and the sciences. The center could offer programs on what it was like to be an undergraduate science major, as well as on other science-related topics—lectures on gender bias in health research and funding; conversations with practicing women scientists about career development; and examinations of the gendered nature of epidemics like AIDS.

However, I was not satisfied to include science students and faculty in women's studies only as a potential audience. I wanted to involve them more directly in the initiation and organization of science projects. I decided to try to create a new group, Women in Science. By encouraging science faculty and students to take ownership of the center's science focus, my thought was that Women in Science could provide a strong link between women's studies and the sciences.

To get the new group off the ground, I enlisted the help of two student assistants, Vicky and Jeanette, who were both majoring in biology. By the end of the fall semester, they had sent letters inviting every undergraduate woman science major and every member of the science faculty to an organizational meeting of Women in Science. I had high hopes when I walked into the room and saw more than forty students and faculty, many of whom had had no previous contact with women's studies.

I had asked Vicky to facilitate the meeting. Well aware of how important it would be to Women in Science's success, I prepared her carefully. I explained that she should try to create as open a discussion as possible, while at the same time making sure that certain basic questions were addressed: whether an organization like Women in Science was needed, what functions it might fulfill, and how it should be organized. If the group were to be affiliated with women's studies, it would have to be more than a social group or women's science club. It would need an explicitly academic focus. What I hoped would emerge was a group that could encourage the serious exploration of gender issues in the sciences, a group that could help reassure students like Anna and faculty like Professor Agee that their feminism was compatible with the pursuit of a scientific career.

None of that happened. The meeting was a disaster. Vicky began well enough, introducing herself and then briefly explaining what the center did and how it was organized. But when she opened the floor to suggestions about the purpose of Women in Science, the silence was heavy. As is often the case at a first meeting, everyone seemed reluctant to speak. Instead of waiting in the knowledge that no matter how long it takes, eventually someone will say something, Vicky panicked. Out came her own ideas about what Women in Science should do.

> It would be so great if we could sit around informally and talk about the stuff that bothers us as women. We could discuss things like menstruation and relationships, and how we feel about being women. Teachers and students could share what we have in common. It would be great to have a support group like that.

I could not believe that Vicky was describing exactly the kind of group I wanted to avoid. Looking around the room, I saw people shifting in their chairs as they glanced uncomfortably at one another or stared at the floor. I knew that every negative stereotype of women's studies they had ever heard was being confirmed. Because they assumed that Vicky's views represented the center, I had little doubt that they would want no part of Women in Science.

Desperate to salvage the situation, I interrupted Vicky to report that an eminent physicist from Cornell University had already agreed to kick off Women in Science by leading a Brown Bag discussion at the center on careers in physics for women. Deliberately continuing to ignore Vicky, I asked the group for names of other scientists from whom they would like to hear, and for topics they would like addressed. But even as I spoke I saw that most of the audience had already made up their minds that Women in Science was not for them. I watched as the fledgling organization disappeared before my eyes.

Later, several faculty who had attended the meeting confirmed my impression. Professor Ursom, a member of the geology department and a supporter of women's studies, was dismayed at the turn the meeting had taken:

> It's hopeless, I'm afraid. The students who came to that meeting were pretty skeptical of women's studies in the first place, but they thought they'd give it a chance. Several of them have already told me that they won't come back. They think the center is only interested in "touchy-feely stuff." These students tend to be very serious about science and wanted an organization that was equally serious. I know you wanted to create that, but the damage has already been done.

I knew she was right. A month later when the center sponsored a panel discussion about gender bias in NIH funding for cancer research, I was disappointed but not really surprised when only five students and two faculty members showed up. I finally faced the fact that Women in Science was completely dead when not one of them remained after the panel ended to talk about trying to revitalize the group.

It was clear that I would have to proceed without a separate organization if I wanted to create a science focus within women's studies. I decided therefore to simply incorporate science programming into the center's regular schedule. I hoped that over time I would be able to win back the goodwill of science students and faculty. And in fact that is what happened. After a slow beginning, women's studies science programs increasingly attracted good turnouts. Over the years, the center invited many women scientists to lecture, organized panel discussions with Colgate science faculty, and brought local high school girls to campus for a discussion of careers in science. In 1997 at the initiative of a student assistant, the center sponsored five full days of science-related projects and programs during a designated "Gender and Science Week." Programs on science and gender had become a regular feature of the center.

Of these programs, two lectures by feminist philosophers of science raised the most interesting issues concerning science, women, and feminism. The approaches of Tamara Horowitz and Laura Reutsche were similar. Both addressed the question of women's historical underrepresentation in the physical sciences by exploring the basic issue of whether women could and should do science.

Both of them rejected out of hand the claim that women are incapable of thinking scientifically, an argument they described as the traditional explanation for women's near absence among great scientists. Instead, they offered a sociological interpretation. It was, they claimed, the omnipresence of obstacles that society and the scientific professions have placed in women's paths that have blocked their full participation in the sciences. They cited three major obstacles: gender discrimination in hiring and promotion, a sexist socialization and educational process that associates science with masculinity, and the demanding and inflexible nature of scientific careers that makes them difficult to reconcile with child and home responsibilities.

In her lecture, Professor Reutsche also addressed the question of whether women should even do science. Some feminists, she noted, believe that women have been right to reject science because it is inherently masculine. This feminist antiscience position claims that science is aggressive, destructive, and misogynist. It is on that basis, they argue, that women have repudiated and should avoid the discipline as a whole. Professor Reutsche herself strongly rejected this position, explaining in detail why she believed that it made no sense to argue that science was inherently gendered.

Her denial triggered a vigorous debate following her remarks. Several Colgate faculty members made precisely the argument that Professor Reutsche had been at pains to disavow: that science was inherently masculine. Professor Cornett, a member of the physics department, was the most explicit. "When I am doing science," he said, "I am using my masculine side, but when I am falling in love, I am using my feminine side. Why fight it? Women obviously [are] more feminine than masculine."

Professor Reutsche, herself a physicist as well as a philosopher, looked incredulous. "You're a scientist," she replied. "But what you just said can't be backed up with even a shred of evidence. You would never be so cavalier about method and evidence in a physics lab. Why do you think you can create theories about masculinity and femininity without even attempting to test them? That's not science." Professor Reutsche went on to point out that his view that science is masculine was bound to have the effect of discouraging women from thinking they could be great scientists. As such, Professor Cornett had just provided an illustration of what stood in the way of women's doing science.

A similar exchange occurred in the discussion following Professor Horowitz's lecture. In her presentation, she had spent considerable time refuting the claim that women and men are intellectually dissimilar—that they think differently and that the way they do science is fundamentally different. In response, Professor Lauerman, a member of Colgate's philosophy department, took exception. Echoing sentiments similar to Professor Cornett's, she stated: "I am a strong feminist, and I believe that doing science is not the same for everyone. Because I am a woman, I think about things without a masculinist bias. My consciousness is different than a man's, so if I did science it would be more feminine, too." Professor Horowitz disagreed, strongly denying that Professor Lauerman could show that, as actually practiced, women and men do science any differently. If presented with examples of the work of men and women scientists without identifying the authors, she said, it would be impossible to distinguish between them on the basis of their gender.

Though Women in Science as an organization was a failure, these two lectures and other similar center programs helped to fill the science void in women's studies. The debates on campus that they triggered involved women's studies faculty and students as well as many in the sciences. Through them, women's studies established that science was a legitimate part of its domain. Neither the general view that feminism was antiscience nor that science was inherently sexist easily could be maintained in the face of the dialogue on science established by the center.

I was eager to find a way for women's studies to tap into the interests of the large number of undergraduate women involved in intercollegiate athletics. I hoped to attract these students to women's studies programs that explored the role of gender in sport. From my own work, I knew that this was a rapidly growing research area of feminist scholarship. I thought the center could play a role in encouraging students to think systematically about an area of culture in which they enthusiastically participated, but which they rarely analyzed.

Several of the student assistants working at the center were varsity athletes. Not surprisingly, they were keen on the idea of bringing more athletes into center programs and into women's studies. Kara, a record-setting sprinter on the track team, became the most active, working long and hard to involve athletes in the projects on sports. In the first two years she worked as a student assistant, Kara organized a number of events: center-sponsored "Fun Runs" to raise money for women's sports at Colgate, meetings of team captains to discuss subjects ranging from equity to eating disorders, and a celebration of women's athletic accomplishments as part of Colgate's twenty-fifth anniversary of coeducation.

But through it all Kara was disappointed. Her hoped-for participation by large numbers of women athletes never materialized. With consistently poor turnouts to show for her two years of hard work and persistent organizing, Kara finally threw in the towel at the beginning of her third year as a student assistant. "I've tried everything I can think of," she told me one day, "but I need a new project. I hate to give up, but I can't keep after them any more. It's really hopeless. Women athletes just are too nervous about being identified with women's studies. No matter what the program is, most of them just won't come out to a center-sponsored event."

In our many discussions trying to account for this lack of interest, Kara and other athletes maintained that the main problem was that female athletes were often stigmatized as lesbians. Because of that stereotype, many highly visible female athletes feared an association with women's studies. Since the center was also a target of homophobia, women athletes were concerned that involvement there would doubly tarnish them. To avoid this, many steered clear of the program altogether.

The annual survey of student attitudes conducted by my introductory women's studies classes provided some support for this explanation. The students had included two questions on women and athletics: whether women students could be athletes and also be feminine, and whether Colgate female athletes were more or less feminine than their nonathletic counterparts. A clear difference emerged between male and female respondents. I had not anticipated that women undergraduates would be more likely to find sports and femininity incompatible, but these results were no surprise to my students. It was obvious, they explained to me, that women would worry the most about sports participation depriving them of their femininity. And among women, it was the serious athletes who were most anxious in this regard. One student, a varsity athlete who was also a women's studies major, explained: "Since women's studies is seen by most people as antimale and unfeminine, lots of women athletes I know, especially the ones who are worried about whether they are feminine enough— and that's just about everyone—keep their distance. My friends told me I was crazy to declare this major—that now I'd *really* be seen as a lesbian by everyone."

I reported on all of this to Kara one morning when she arrived early at the center for work. She said it confirmed what she had thought, and she added, "Isn't that depressing?" But in the next breath she was talking about a great book by a lesbian athlete that she had just finished reading. "It's really exciting," she said. "It talked about lots of this stuff. I know I said I was giving up on athletes and women's studies, but why don't we try to bring her to Colgate and at least get the subject out in the open; it might do some good."

Following up on Kara's recommendation, I invited Mariah Burton Nelson to visit the center the following spring. To Kara's delight, Nelson, a former collegiate and professional basketball player, drew a large crowd to her lecture. The title of her most recent book, *The*

Stronger Women Get, the More Men Love Football, had obviously struck a chord.[3] In her talk, Nelson approached the issue of homophobia in women's athletics directly. She described the enormous pressure on female athletes to be feminine in traditionally stereotyped ways in order to avoid a lesbian label. Pointing to the fact that sport is seen by most as masculine, she argued that women athletes are uniformly stereotyped as unfeminine. For too many people, it is only a short step from that to the belief that allegedly masculinized women athletes must also be lesbians. This was the reason, she said, that many female athletes feel that they have to adhere to traditionally feminine patterns of behavior whether they want to or not.

Nelson went on to link women's athletic involvement to feminism. Her view was that athletic participation contributes to self-esteem, independence, and empowerment, and that therefore women who are involved in sports are, by definition, feminists. But, she ironically acknowledged, that very participation sometimes makes female athletes unwilling to identify with the women's movement. Nelson again corroborated Kara and others' view that, for many women athletes, avoidance of feminism (and women's studies) was rooted in their fear of being labeled as gay.

The discussion that followed her remarks was fascinating, as students talked openly about a subject that previously had been taboo. One undergraduate described how she and her friends had been harassed by male students calling them "dykes" as they walked home from soccer practice. Others reported how difficult it was for female athletes to form relationships with college men. A star softball player recounted that during her first semester at Colgate, a male acquaintance expressed shock at seeing her at a fraternity party. "What are you doing here?" he had asked. "I never thought I'd see you looking like this. Isn't the whole softball team gay? I just assumed you were, too." She was so hurt that she left the party in tears.

The students also were eager to talk with Nelson about their grievance that the women's athletic program at Colgate received far less funding and support than did the men's. Kelley, a member of the

3. Mariah Burton Nelson, *The Stronger Women Get, the More Men Love Football: Sexism and the American Culture of Sports* (New York: Avon Books, 1995).

basketball team, volunteered an example: "We get a raw deal. The football team gets steak before their games, but not us. It's just not fair." But it soon became clear that though they were quick to complain about the lack of support women athletes receive, none of the students possessed any real information concerning the distribution of athletic funding at Colgate. Not a single student could answer Nelson's questions about the extent of Colgate's compliance with Title IX, the federal law requiring equality in men's and women's athletic programs.

After the students had left the center, Burton expressed to me her shock at the students' lack of information, and she not so subtly implied that women's studies should have been doing a better job of educating them. I, however, put the responsibility back on the students. I told Nelson that every year the center held discussions on Title IX and its implications. Student attendance was always abysmal. In fact, at the center's panel on athletic equity earlier that very year, the director of athletics not only had offered details about the athletic program, but also had essentially admitted that the college was not in compliance—though the students could not have known that because they were largely absent. Nelson expressed amazement at the resignation with which women undergraduates accepted the problems they faced as athletes at Colgate. "It's so contradictory," she exclaimed in frustration. "They seem committed to athletics and aware of the inequities, yet at the same time are unwilling to do anything to change women's sports."

The irony, however, was that the students were acting in precisely the way that Nelson's own argument would predict. Their pervasive fear of being labeled lesbians, as she had indicated, seemed to discourage even those who otherwise might have been interested in pressing for athletic equity. Because of its inevitably feminist overtones, a militant campaign on behalf of women's athletics was likely to frighten off most women athletes.

Furthermore, Nelson's definition of feminism was of no use in reversing the students' political quietism. Her view that taking part in athletic activity was enough to define a woman as a feminist made no demand for a political or collective engagement. Feminism in this view required only individual lifestyle choices and cultural participation. I pointed out to Nelson that her approach actually reinforced students' reluctance to engage in activism. After all, she had assured them that simply being an athlete was feminist empowerment. Though unintended, Nelson's message legitimated the students' predisposition to emphasize individual choices in defining their feminism and to remain passive in the face of inequities.

It was not as if no opportunities for activism were present on the campus. There was, for example, a long-standing and highly publicized lawsuit brought by alumnae seeking to establish a women's varsity ice hockey team. Whenever I asked undergraduates in my classes about the case, however, I drew a blank. They had heard, as a student in one class put it, "something about a suit," but my raising it failed typically to evoke much interest. One day after discussing the women's ice hockey situation in some detail, I asked my upper-level class on "Women and Social Change" whether Colgate students should support the hockey team's suit. An unusually long silence indicated their discomfort with my question. Finally, Penny, a senior on the lacrosse team, spoke up: "Well, I guess they have a right to sue, but they aren't being very loyal to Colgate. It really makes the school look bad." Another student, Alice, who constantly bemoaned the "second-class treatment" of women athletes at Colgate, agreed with Penny: "We really don't have enough information, do we? Anyhow, no one wants to get everyone on campus mad at them."

This combination of dissatisfaction with the status of women's sports, on the one hand, and a decided reluctance to do anything to try to change that status, on the other, revealed itself in other contexts as well. In an introductory class where we were exploring policies that might reduce the gender inequity in sport, I suggested that the promotion of coed sports was one way to achieve equality for women. This model would be to separate individuals irrespective of gender into teams based on their ability, weight, or height. To my surprise only one student, Maggie, agreed with this idea. "I can tell you from my experience that it would work," she said in endorsement. "The only reason I am as good an athlete as I am is that I grew up playing sports with my five older brothers. The competition was great. I really learned to take it! There's no reason in the world that boys and girls shouldn't play sports together." But everyone else in the class strongly objected. Samantha dismissed the idea on the grounds that it would be too complicated to implement and administer. Deb claimed that because of differences in size and ability, men and women would end up on different teams anyway, "so why bother." And Rachel worried about the fact that girls would become "as aggressive, unfair, and competitive as boys." But the comment that seemed to resonate the most with the other students was Johanna's; she argued that coed sports would ultimately harm women. "I don't want to be on the same team with them," she declared. "I could never keep up. Even if it made me strong to compete against men, I'd never get the chance to be the best on the team. Then I'd *really* only be second class." Beneath the resistance to coed sports for many was the belief that women are so different from—and at least in athletics so much inferior to—men that they would always be at a competitive disadvantage. As a result, most of my students chose the continued existence of a protected, if underfunded, enclave in which they would only have to compete with one another— separate and unequal.

A conflict similar to the one between the students' desire for equity and their simultaneous fear that they would lose out if they were to compete directly with men is found in much of feminist thought. It partially accounts for a bedrock disagreement among feminists that has continued since the inception of the first wave of the women's movement. On one side are those who have advocated protectionist legislation for women, and on the other are those who have wanted so- cial policy to be based on strict equality between women and men.[4] The inability to resolve this ambivalence puts feminism in the untenable position of both wanting and at the same time denying the possibility of equality. This ambivalence characterized Penny's final comment on Colgate's athletic scene: "I get so mad when I go to Huntington [Colgate's gym] and the boys won't let me play. I'm better than half of them. But I wouldn't want to be on the same court with them because they play so dirty. I'd get killed."

Penny did, but I did not, count it a victory when soon thereafter the athletic department implemented a new policy in response to complaints by women athletes concerning court time. The intention

4. Wendy Kaminer, *A Fearful Freedom: Women's Flight from Equality* (Reading, Mass.: Addison-Wesley, 1990).

was to be more fair to women by providing them with increased access to the court. But this was not to be done by requiring that pickup ball be coed. Instead, official signs appeared, decorating the gym and designating Wednesdays as "women's basketball night." The signs were all bright pink.

It was important to me that Colgate's women's studies program connect with feminism off the campus in order to provide the students with insights into the contemporary women's movement. I wanted them to see directly how what they studied in the classroom actually played out in the rest of the world. Because Colgate is rural and therefore isolated, students could not easily make such contacts themselves. So each year the center organized trips to statewide and national feminist conventions and gatherings, women's studies conferences at other universities, and to the state capital, Albany, for briefings with feminist advocates, lobbyists, and legislators. In addition, we arranged for firsthand observation of local family courts, nearby shelters, and community groups.

One such trip involved participation in a two-day conference on global feminism called "Bringing Beijing Home," organized by women's studies at the State University of New York at New Paltz (SUNY). As part of the arrangements, students at New Paltz agreed to host the Colgate undergraduates, putting them up overnight. In addition to the conference, this, too, turned out to be an important learning experience.

SUNY is a public university that at New Paltz draws a large number of students from New York City and environs; Colgate, on the other hand, is private and more academically selective, with many students who grew up in suburbs and small towns. There were other differences between the two groups of students as well. Almost all the SUNY students involved were senior women's studies majors living in off-campus apartments. The center-sponsored Colgate students were younger, most lived in dorms on campus, and only a few were women's studies majors. Unlike the SUNY students, who were active in campus feminist organizations, many in the Colgate group were experiencing their first involvement with women's studies or the center.

The twenty-three Colgate students and I arrived at New Paltz late on a Friday evening and, after some difficulty, located the apartment where we were to meet our hosts for the weekend. As we wound our way up the four flights of narrow steps of a noisy, dilapidated apartment building, I could feel tension rising among the students. Entering the apartment, my group's nervousness turned to silence. The Colgate students stood huddled together on one side of the apartment, staring at the twelve SUNY students, who stood on the other side of the living room, staring back. Each group was in uniform: it was the punks versus the preppies. The SUNY students had closely cropped hair dyed a rainbow of colors from blue to orange; multiple nose, ear, and lip rings; and ripped jeans. Every single Colgate student had long, carefully coifed hair and was dressed as if she had just stepped out of the pages of a J. Crew or Eddie Bauer catalog.

I broke the silence by thanking the SUNY students for inviting us, and I suggested that we each give our names and say something about ourselves. The students dutifully complied, but this icebreaking exercise did little to ease the discomfort that was palpable in the room. After a brief discussion of logistics, the Colgate students—with worried backward glances at their friends—divided up and awkwardly walked off with their hosts. I was far from convinced that the students in either group would be willing to overcome the negative image each obviously held of the other—at least long enough to talk about what they might have in common.

But when I met my students for breakfast the next morning, I thought, at first, that my fears were unjustified. They were falling over one another in their eagerness to talk about their overnight experiences. "They're so cool!" said Fran of the two students in whose apartment she, Marilyn, and Alis had stayed. "They've been everywhere and done everything. They talked all night about their group on campus that fights violence against women. I want to start one at Colgate as soon as we get back." Then Alis chimed in: "It was awesome. None of us ever really had a chance to meet radical lesbians before." Jan, who had stayed in a different apartment, also reported being fascinated by her hosts. But she said her feelings had been hurt when the SUNY students were critical of her and the other Colgate students for not majoring in women's studies. "They kept on pushing us. They said we couldn't really be committed to feminism unless we majored. When I told them I planned to use a feminist perspective when I teach high school English, they said majoring in English was a cop out for anyone who really cared about women."

Helen and Maria had yet another tale. They were upset because their host had been so unfriendly. "She didn't want to talk. We tried, but it was obvious that she wasn't interested in anything about us at all," Maria explained. Maureen, who had stayed in the same apartment, agreed. "But the worst thing," she continued, "was that whenever any of us said a word she thought was sexist—even when we were talking to each other—she fined us a quarter. When anyone said 'you guys' or 'chairman' or 'history' instead of 'herstory,' we got fined. It really was annoying. But what really got to me was what happened this morning when Helen and I tried to give her instructions to drive us to our van." Helen continued the story: "When we got in the car, I said, 'Just go straight.' The words 'go straight' completely flipped her out. She and her friend were furious at me. They fined me seventy-five cents—one for each word—and kept talking about how homophobic some people are—meaning us of course. But I'm not. I only meant they shouldn't turn off the street we were on!"

It turned out that all the Colgate students had been subject to fining. Some of them, however, were reluctant to be critical of the SUNY students. "It's not like they were picking on us. They fine each other for sexist language, too, you know. It was all in fun," said Eve. "Anyhow, they're so radical." Meg interjected: "I thought it was kind of stupid, but they do have a point. How you say things is important. Actually I wouldn't have minded if they would use the money for something good, instead of just for beer."

While the students recounted their experiences of the night before, I noticed that Rhonda, a senior women's studies major who was usually talkative, remained off by herself. After breakfast I sought her out to find out whether she was all right. At first she denied that anything was wrong, but soon she told me what had her so upset. She had stayed alone with two SUNY students in their tiny one-room apartment. After what she thought was a good talk with them, Rhonda had fallen asleep in a sleeping bag on the floor near the one bed in the apartment. "It didn't bother me at all that they were sleeping in the same bed—no big deal," she said. "They were obviously lovers." What did bother her, however, was that the students completely ignored her feelings and had loud and frequent sex together for the better part of the rest of the night. "It was like they were showing off in some way or trying to hurt my feelings because I'm heterosexual," said Rhonda. "Maybe it was just immature of them, but I was only a couple of feet from their bed. It was really rude."

In the van on the way back to Colgate after the conference, the conversation indicated that most students were still in awe of the SUNY undergraduates, whose in-your-face brand of feminism to them seemed courageous and daring. A few were mildly critical of the SUNY students' intolerance. But even they surrounded their reproaches with caveats, justifying it as "really feminist." Only Donna boldly stated her disapproval. "You're wrong to excuse them," she declared to the others. "The whole time, they looked down on us as not being feminist enough. They never gave us a chance to really say what our ideas were. Why do you think that's so radical? I don't. They think they have all the answers, and they don't really care what anyone else thinks."

On another off-campus trip the following year, some of these same students attended the New York State NOW convention. This trip put Colgate students in contact with a different group of feminists, nonstudents who were part of a serious national political organization working for social change. Again, the Colgate students stood out as different. They were by far the youngest participants, and they were not members of NOW. But they were eagerly welcomed and were urged to participate in discussion sessions and workshops. They were even invited to sit in on the business meeting as observers.

Every minute of the convention seemed to present the Colgate students with something new. Instead of the academic discussions of feminism they were used to, they were confronted at the convention by hundreds of women actually hammering out policies designed to eliminate sexism. The students were amazed at the diversity of the group and impressed by the number of points of view concerning where the women's movement should go and what role NOW could play. Patricia Ireland, NOW's president, seemed to speak directly to the Colgate students when, in her keynote address, she stressed how crucial the input of young women was to NOW. Though the convention's general focus was on grassroots organizing and politics, the program itself was varied. Bella and Geena for example, two women who had been active feminists for more than thirty years, read a long poem they had written to their families and children explaining why they had recently become lovers. Other women spoke of the history of the women's movement that had inspired them to get involved with NOW. The students also had an opportunity to hear Barbara Ehrenreich, whose books many of them had read for their classes.

The presence of so many well-known feminists, the exciting process of people actually "doing feminism" (as one student put it), and the attention given to them was both exhilarating and flattering to the students. "It was wonderful to see so many different women so committed," said Davida on the way back to Colgate. "I really didn't know anything about NOW before this. It does some fantastic things." However, when I prompted them to think critically about what they had seen and heard, the students were reticent. "I thought it was all so great," said Jennifer. "Besides, do we really have a right to criticize them when they've done so much? They're the pioneers who made it possible for us. What have we done?"

Concerned at the students' unwillingness to analyze what they had heard and seen at the convention, I called a meeting a week later to give those who had attended another chance to talk through their experience. When only positive comments were again offered, I tried to provoke them: "Can it be that you all agreed with every word you heard? That's seems pretty implausible, doesn't it?" I reassured them that they would not be rejecting feminism or being disrespectful to older feminists if they voiced criticism. Slowly, a few students overcame their hesitation. "Don't get me wrong," began Linda defensively. "I thought Bella and Geena were terrific. It really took courage for them, at the age of seventy or whatever, to do what they did. But I have to admit that I really didn't like some of their poem. It was pretty bitter. Their idea that men run the world in order to try to control women because they are jealous of our uteruses was a bit much. I just don't think that it makes sense to exaggerate like that."

Kathee, a junior women's studies major who had been especially excited about hearing Ehrenreich, a writer she had long admired, also spoke up. She began by praising Ehrenreich's focus on society's demonization of welfare recipients: "People are always accusing feminists of being selfish and only caring about themselves. I think it's cool that she writes about welfare moms." But Kathee conceded that she had some criticisms as well. She questioned Ehrenreich's statement that no one has the right to tell welfare recipients that they should limit the number of children they have. Ehrenreich had said that feminists should support poor women's decisions to have as many children as they want. "Of course I agree with the idea of reproductive choice," said Kathee, "but I don't think women, on welfare or not, should decide to have kids without thinking about the consequences."

Dolores said she was thinking of joining NOW, explaining, "They need some young people to get active." Jo agreed: "I love the fact that NOW deals with real-life issues with real live people. That's what I liked about the convention—it really puts what I believe into practice." But others were skeptical. Reacting to a workshop in which NOW members enthusiastically discussed new strategies to pass an Equal Rights Amendment (ERA), Sheena questioned whether the organization should give so much attention to an issue that most young people felt was dead. "I'm not sure I can get motivated about the ERA, so if that's going to be their focus I probably won't join." Robin, too, expressed doubts. At the convention she had listened to a long discussion that had been critical of the wording of NOW's original 1966 goal of "bringing women into the mainstream . . . in a truly equal partnership with men." Robin questioned how many new members NOW would be able to attract if they rejected being part of the mainstream. She concluded, "I want to wait and see what they actually decide."

Whether the students decided to join or not, I could see that being at the NOW convention had broadened their view of feminism and helped them to find their voice. They realized that they had ideas they could express. June reflected this new confidence when she summarized her reaction to the meeting. "I was really amazed that I could hold my own. I understood what people were talking about, and I had some things to contribute myself. People actually listened to me when I talked about the apathy toward feminism on campuses and what I thought we could do about that. I never realized I could make a difference in a real feminist organization."

From the beginning, I insisted that center programming include an international focus. I wanted the students to develop an understanding of women and gender beyond their own society. But I found them oddly ambivalent about discussing the changing lives of women in other countries. Their curiosity about women elsewhere was genuine. They listened with interest to descriptions about how other women lived. But when prompted to discuss issues concerning gender or feminism in other societies, they clammed up. Especially where the lives of women in poor countries were concerned, and where critical thought was called for, they routinely refused to engage in analysis at all.

The issue of global feminism was the subject of the first Brown Bag in the fall semester of 1995. I had chosen the topic of the Fourth United Nations International Conference on Women partially because extensive media coverage had stimulated interest in the recently concluded Beijing meeting. After showing a short film depicting the enthusiastic reaction of a delegation of American women to the conference, I offered some comments to start the discussion. I described how the conference had revealed growing global concern about domestic violence, women's legal rights, reproductive choice, economic opportunities, and the worldwide neglect of girls' and women's health care and education. All of these issues constituted common bonds among the thousands of women at the Beijing conference. The meeting itself and the publicity it attracted, I argued, served not only to raise awareness around the world, but also to provide the basis for coordinated efforts at change. It legitimated and supported the efforts of feminists everywhere to fight practices and policies harmful to women.

The hostile tone of the discussion that followed was not at all what I expected. Several members of the audience spoke directly against changes occurring in women's lives, and strongly objected to the Beijing conference on the grounds that it would accelerate the process of change. Professor Easterlin, for example, challenged the legitimacy of the demands for change developed by conference participants. "The delegates to Beijing were well-educated women who have been overly influenced by Western ideas," she declared. "How do they know whether women really want the birth control, laws against battering, and education of girls that these delegates are advocating? Where are the poor rural women? Who knows what they want?" A student spoke up, agreeing with Professor Easterlin. "Really," she argued, "as white middle-class American women, we have no right to approve of what went on at Beijing. With our Western bias, we can't possibly understand what women's lives are like in other cultures, or what they are going through." Terry, a history major and student assistant at the center, went even further, announcing that she thought the conference was dangerous and harmful to the world's women. "This is just another instance of Western countries trying to impose their values and ideas on other people. Just like when the Jesuits came to Central America," Terry continued, "pretending they wanted to educate the native peoples, but actually exploiting them and robbing them of their own culture and traditions. Western feminists are doing the same thing to women."

I was not the only one at the Brown Bag floored by this attack on the Beijing conference. Professor Flowers of the economics department spoke out in its defense: "The Beijing meetings were all about choice. They were about helping women everywhere to have more options than they did before, to decide for themselves the roles and lives they lead, rather than be controlled by tradition, men, or restrictive customs." Her words, however, did little to placate Terry, who immediately retorted, "Choice is a Western concept. Who says women want these choices? In most places choice isn't even part of people's vocabulary. We don't have the right to add it and disrespect their traditions and cultures." That proved too much for Professor Flowers. Looking right at Terry, she slowly and deliberately responded, "Terry, I'm not sure you understand the conservative implications of what you are saying. Do you see that if you reject the kind of changes, including basic education, that offer women choices, that things will stay the same? How can you say you want women to remain forever inferior?"

If ever there was a polarizing issue, this was it. Most everyone at the Brown Bag lined up on one side or the other. One group took the position that even discussing global feminism was illegitimate. To them, it was only a vehicle for Westerners and educated elites to illegitimately impose their ideas on poor women. On the other side were those like me with the conviction that everyone has not only the right but also the responsibility to speak out against injustices wherever they exist. "Why," I asked, "should the education and access to birth control we have struggled for in this country not also be made available to others elsewhere? Why shouldn't we criticize the leaders of countries that deny these to women?"

But I had not gauged accurately just how deep was the impulse to abstain from criticism. Many in the audience had real difficulty in finding fault even with female infanticide when this issue was raised. Terry, Professor Easterlin, and several others, though not without obvious discomfort, remained firm that—even on this issue—judging other societies was simply wrong. Their default position was one part pleading ignorance and one part claiming false humility. Terry put it succinctly: "I'm not sure we really know enough about what is going on in other cultures to decide. Anyhow, knowing that I am from the West, I'm just not comfortable saying yes or no about anything."

It was obvious that, for many students and faculty, cultural relativism had become the order of the day. They would simply not allow themselves to evaluate any cultural practice that was not their own. What they vigorously condemned in their own society did not evoke a similar outrage when it occurred elsewhere. It was not lack of concern that motivated this refusal to engage; they did care about what was happening to women in other societies. But somehow they had become convinced that it was disrespectful and therefore illegitimate for them as Americans to approve or disapprove of how others lived. Even if they did have such opinions, as I suspect they must have, they thought they should not articulate them. To comment on others, they believed, was to bully them—to impose their will on less powerful people. So instead, when thinking about women in other societies, they suspended both their critical intellect and their sense of morality.

A similar issue arose again the following fall. As I drove back to Colgate with the group of students who had attended the New Paltz "Bringing Beijing Home" conference, we talked about the meeting's major theme: how to implement the Beijing conference's goals in the United States. On this subject, the students were talkative and enthusiastic, with many ideas and opinions. But when the conversation turned to global feminism, an issue that also had been prominently discussed at the conference, a tense hush enveloped the van. Finally, Becky spoke up, repeating the refrain I had heard so often: "How can I, an American with all my privileges, say whether women in the third world are really oppressed?" I knew that Becky was reacting to a particularly sharp exchange that had occurred at the conference at a panel on genital mutilation in Africa. One speaker, a women's studies professor at New Paltz, had strongly criticized those who condemned that practice. She insisted that genital mutilation was something with which feminists in the United States should not concern themselves. A second panelist, a delegate to the Beijing conference, took the opposite position, vehemently arguing that feminists at that meeting had been right to speak out against a dangerous ritual.

Of the two, it was the first speaker who really impressed the students. Her words reinforced those who, like Becky, already believed that women in the United States should not comment on the lives of women in other parts of the world. "There's plenty of domestic violence and discrimination against women in the United States today to worry about," Becky said. "I think we ought to concentrate on that instead of sticking our noses in other people's business where it isn't wanted." I could not help but note the irony that Becky, a women's studies major who had forceful opinions on everything even remotely connected to women, thought that on this subject she should be agnostic.

I pursued the point, and in so doing kept a promise I had made ten years earlier, after teaching for a semester in the People's Republic of China. As I left that country, my female students there had begged me to be unsparing in reporting on their exploited status in Chinese society. They knew that international contacts and support were essential if they were to be able to pursue their fight to achieve justice for themselves and other Chinese women.

I told my Colgate students about my classroom translator, Ping Yau-chen, with whom I had worked closely. Ping was a graduate student in sociology who habitually risked herself at the university by speaking out against the inequalities between women and men that surrounded her. She had explained to me that men were routinely favored at every level of the university. The same was true after graduation. Men got the best jobs. As students, Ping and her women friends found themselves confronting a university bureaucracy that every day unthinkingly demonstrated its belief in male superiority. She reported that the only time the administration would pay any attention to their grievances was when they were able to point beyond China to the existence of a worldwide feminist movement. "It really helps a lot," Ping would tell me, "that outside of China there is so much support for equal education for women."

As if the second-class status they experienced at the university and the economic discrimination they would meet in their careers were not sufficient, my Chinese women students also faced intense pressure to marry as soon as possible. "I love to study and I don't want to think about getting married," confided Reuan, "but I know I must, as my parents say, because no woman can survive here without a husband. Remaining single isn't a possibility." But they also knew that their problems had only just begun even if they conceded to social pressure and sought husbands. These young women understood that they were too educated to be attractive to tradition-minded Chinese men. "I have a graduate degree," lamented Ping. "No one wants to marry such a serious woman. Who knows who I'll have to end up with?"

As if to corroborate Ping's worry, one day in class a male student elicited loud applause from the other men in my course on the Chinese family when he stood up and declared, "I would never marry too educated a woman. I want someone who will take care of me, but an educated girl will have ideas of her own. I need a simple girl. She must be pretty and young and agreeable." While educated women in China suffered many fewer disadvantages than Chinese women had in the past—after all, foot-binding, female infanticide, and officially arranged marriages are, at least according to the law, no longer allowed—being a woman, as Ping told me in the American slang she so often used, "was still double-trouble." I concluded my story by telling the Colgate students that I felt sure Ping would be disappointed to learn that American women were reluctant to support her efforts. She would have trouble believing that they had a double standard: that they believed in the fight for women's rights in the United States, but they reserved judgment about whether that fight for equality was legitimate in China.

By the time we drove up to the Center for Women's Studies, I was thoroughly unnerved. For despite my long recitation about China,

Becky and the others had remained unmoved by what I had said. All they would do was continue to reiterate their cliché: "But we have such different cultures."

Recognizing both my students' cultural parochialism and my own enthusiasm for the increase in global efforts for women's equity, I decided to create a new course. I introduced "International Perspectives on Women and Social Change" as the biyearly topic of the women's studies senior seminar. It occurred to me that perhaps the widespread reluctance among students to address women's lives elsewhere stemmed partially from their lack of information about societies other than their own. It could be that when they said "we can't know different cultures," what they really meant was that they themselves in fact knew little about them. I hoped that the course's intensive study of women's lives in other countries would help overcome that ignorance.

As the semester began, I again faced what I had encountered before: a reluctance to make judgments about other women, and claims that "Western bias" makes it impossible to understand other societies. Myra took the most extreme position. She had spent the previous semester in India. Before leaving on her trip, we had talked at some length about her idea for a research project on the lives of adolescent Indian village girls. She was enthusiastic about it, and promised to keep me informed. I thought it odd that I had not heard from Myra all fall. So at the first meeting of the seminar, the January after she returned, I asked what had happened. Myra's explanation was that she had given up the research project shortly after arriving in India. "I would have had to ask them all kinds of questions," she said. "I decided that that was really unfair. What gave me the right to find out about their lives? It kind of made me feel, well, like I was being colonialistic."

In seminar, Myra continued to insist that it was a form of imperialism to try to learn about people living in less developed societies. Though others did not go that far, there was definite skepticism about the course material, and several students argued that they did not trust the scholarly work I had assigned them to read. Analytic academic research was suspect. My students thought it could not accurately portray the lives of ordinary women who were so different from the researchers themselves. The only literature they thought legitimate was by those who wrote, as they often put it, "from their own personal, lived experience."

I rejected this intellectual nihilism. I told the students that outside of class they could think anything they wanted, but that in the seminar they were each to become an expert on the changing lives of women in a country of their choice. Their thesis would require extensive reading of work by male and female experts both within and outside that society and not just firsthand accounts. In particular, I wanted them to explore the disagreements that emerged among authors. They would also have to provide empirical measures of changes in women's status, including, for example, women's employment, education, and political participation. Finally, though I knew they would be uncomfortable doing so, I insisted that each student make reasoned judgments about the lives of the women she was studying. Each thesis had to assess the hypothesis that the changes they had documented benefited women.

For the second seminar meeting of the semester, I invited Professor Desai, a visiting professor who I knew to be a strong advocate of global feminism, to speak. I told her the concerns that students had expressed the previous week. As a result, she devoted her lecture to championing the legitimacy of studying, critiquing, and judging other women's lives. She strongly condemned traditional sexist customs that hurt women in many non-Western societies, including her own country of origin, India. Of the recent Taliban victory in Afghanistan she cautioned:

> Sexism always tries to hide behind the cloak of tradition. Men in power use the idea of tradition to keep women dependent and in the home—to deny them the freedom given to men. These traditionalists are hypocrites! They are calling for tradition for women, while they wear jeans and Chicago Bulls T-shirts, and ride around in Toyota trucks, shooting off uzis. What's traditional about that? Tradition for them is just an excuse to make sure they have all the advantages and that women stay suppressed.

After that, the atmosphere in the seminar changed. Professor Desai's words had had an impact. So too did the students' research and reading. They were beginning to accumulate, and share with each other in seminar, information about women's lives in countries around the globe. Increasingly, they came to appreciate the significant commonalities among women that cut across cultural differences. As the students learned more, they became willing to argue with one another, to offer their own opinions and interpretations—in short, to think. With increased familiarity, a good number of them began to identify with women whose practices and lives had previously seemed so different. In addition, expressions of feminism by women in those countries, ideas that many students had earlier claimed were imposed from the West, became more comprehensible as the responses of real women to the actual circumstances of their own lives.

Their thesis presentations at the end of the semester were fascinating. True, several prefaced their papers with the disclaimer that they had no personal experience with the country they had studied, and thus had had to rely only on others' reports. But in class on those rare occasions when someone went further and refused to analyze or judge a situation, offering the "difference" excuse as a defense, it was the other students who objected. They had come to believe that studying, critiquing, and stating their opinions was not the same as imposing their views or coercing behavior in others. A number of the students who had begun the semester thinking it arrogant to judge others were by the end engaged in arguing about the extent to which increased longevity, control of reproduction, better education and health care, and income-earning ability had improved women's lives. They eagerly monitored the details of "their" countries' progress in implementing the goals agreed upon in Beijing, and they unapologetically defended the changes that had come about as a result.

Each year on March 8, the center sponsored a celebration of International Women's Day (IWD). Recognition of the importance of this day was special for me because it captured what I believed was the best of feminism: women from all over the world uniting to advance the cause of justice. The first time I had heard of IWD was in 1976, when I was living and teaching in Guyana. There, it was marked by a countrywide celebration. Though two decades later it was still often ignored in the United States, I wanted Colgate students and faculty to share in the excitement of observing this important day for women.

I had a second motive as well. I hoped that a day honoring both women's commonality and their diversity might be a vehicle for building bridges among women at Colgate. By providing a special occasion for women's studies to work closely with students of all ethnicities, a joint celebration of IWD might help to overcome the reluctance of many women of color to actively participate in the program.

When I first arrived at Colgate, I had assumed that, with a concerted effort, women's studies would be able to attract a wide diversity of students. I was aware of the problems that existed; as early as 1988, the outside review of the women's studies program commented on the absence of women of color. The reviewers criticized what they saw as the program's narrow focus. Complaining about its emphasis on "American middle-class white women," the report concluded that

> the program needs to make more self-conscious efforts to supple-
> ment and internationalize the perspective of white middle-class
> American academic women—and to institute ways of working
> with the Afro-American faculty to enrich their courses. Most ex-
> isting courses in the women's studies curriculum could benefit
> from a greater sensitivity to the different race and class make-up
> in combination with gender.

Whatever the case had been when the report was written, by 1991 when I became director, most women's studies courses regularly included attention to race and class in addition to gender. At the center, too, I made sure that the library included a large collection of materials on and by African American women and other women of color. Student-assistant projects that first year also included attempts at increased diversity—a cross-ethnic discussion group, Women for a Common Understanding, and a black women's film festival.

Despite these efforts, very few women of color were involved either at the center or in women's studies courses. This self-exclusion troubled not only me but also many women's studies students. Each fall when I asked the student assistants at the center what they wanted to work on during the coming year, improving race relations on campus was always a high priority. Shera was typical in explaining why she thought something needed to be done.

> I hate it that black and white women are so divided on this
> campus. It's insane. There's an African American girl here who

went to high school with me. We were really friendly then; we even took a women's studies class together. But now that we're here, it seems like we don't even know each other. When she sees me alone she always says hi, but if she is with anyone else, she just ignores me. It really hurts. Maybe if we could get a project going at the center where everyone could sit down and talk about this stuff, things might be better.

Most of the white students I talked to blamed themselves for the racial tensions on campus. They felt confused and guilty that everything they tried to do to heal the breach had failed. Several African American speakers invited to Colgate by the center had reinforced those feelings. Rebecca Walker, for example, had opened her remarks on the development of the third wave of feminism with an impassioned denunciation of the hundred students in her audience. "Why are there so many white faces in the audience tonight. Where are your African American sisters?" she asked rhetorically. "Why aren't they here?" The students squirmed in their seats. No one dared suggest that the absent black students had chosen for themselves not to attend, and that the students who were present were not responsible for those decisions.

Given this situation, I hoped that a joint celebration of IWD might help ease the tension. How wrong I was. When I attempted to obtain cosponsorship for the event from the director of the Cultural Center, a campus group founded by African American students, I was unceremoniously rebuffed. She told me the Cultural Center would be organizing a "separate celebration" of IWD. To my suggestion that we join together in a larger commemoration, she curtly answered, "I think not." So that year, there were two celebrations, a circumstance that called attention to and even reinforced the unfortunate divisions existing between white and nonwhite women on campus. On March 8, I joined the many women's studies students who supported both the Cultural Center's celebration of IWD as well as the one at the Center for Women's Studies.

The following fall, I again approached the director of the Cultural Center, arguing for a second time that working toward a joint celebration the next March would help to set a tone of cooperation and unity among female undergraduates on campus. This time she agreed. We decided that a combined committee of students from both centers should plan and implement a single celebration.

During the year, however, the combined committee proved to be a disaster. The five students from the Center for Women's Studies who had volunteered to work on the IWD project were completely frustrated. Students from the Cultural Center rarely attended the monthly planning meetings. Phone calls to the director and discussions with students on the committee did nothing to alter the pattern. Then, at the final planning meeting in late February, things changed. A full complement of students from the Cultural Center were in attendance. I was not present, but my intern reported that the Cultural Center students completely took over the meeting, insisting that the planning and publicity for the event be left to them. When others objected, they accused them of not being sensitive to the needs of women of color. In response, the students from the Center for Women's Studies backed down and refused to further object to their exclusion. They were left with no role in what was to have been a joint celebration.

The next day the five Center for Women's Studies students were in my office, trying to make sense of their experience. Barbara, a junior Latin American Studies major from Mexico, was especially distressed. "It's not right. The whole idea was for us all to work together planning the celebration, but that isn't going to happen." When I asked why she had not spoken up at the meeting, she looked embarrassed:

> I felt like they didn't really want us to be part of it. I tried at least to get the celebration held at the Center for Women's Studies, but they didn't like that either. They said women of color wouldn't feel comfortable at the center. I was afraid they would get mad if I pushed. I just didn't want to offend anyone. I hope it comes out okay.

But it did not. The publicity for the event was almost nonexistent. As a result, few attended the celebration other than the thirty or so women students directly associated with the two centers. Once the program started, my frustration over the scanty attendance turned to relief that only a small group had actually come to the celebration. The program arranged by the students from the Cultural Center was a disgrace. After a brief introduction by Cultural Center students outlining the origins of IWD, all mention of women outside the United States completely disappeared from their presentation. Instead, the two student speakers launched an all-out attack on feminism, accusing it of racism and disrespect for African American women. They chastised white women generally and more specifically the white students from the Center for Women's Studies, for "not being able to deal with your own prejudice and racism." In addition, they criticized white feminist scholars, presumably including me, for teaching about the lives of women of color, asserting that for white women to do so was illegitimate. "Until you all acknowledge your racism," they concluded, "we can't be part of your feminism. It will continue to be a white woman's thing."

There was no opportunity for discussion. The program ended abruptly. As we walked back to the Center for Women's Studies, several students were in tears. "I feel so bad," Dierdre whispered. "This was supposed to bring us together, not make things worse. I really don't think I'm a racist, but I don't know how to prove it." But Ingrid was indignant. "Well maybe you're not, but if they say you're a racist, you're stuck. What really gets me is that they didn't even try to work with us. They don't want to hear that feminism is about poor and black and Latina and white, about all women's problems. What do we do now?"

The truth was that I did not have an answer. I did not know how to deal with the guilt and the anger of students on both sides of the conflict. I myself was discouraged at the futility of our attempt to do something about the hostility and hurt of both white and black undergraduates. What I did say, however, was that I wanted us to keep trying to heal these divisions. It was the right thing to say and I believed it, but it was clearly inadequate. I could see that my words did little to reassure them. In good conscience, however, I could offer them nothing more.

The painful racial divisions persisted. Women of color by and large continued to avoid women's studies. African American women twice actually organized their own all-women's group to engage in discussion of what it was like to be black women. But they refused to attach the word *feminist* to these groups, and though I tried to encourage joint meetings with women's studies or the center, none emerged.

Women of color were not alone in blaming feminism for the tensions that existed at Colgate and elsewhere. In my women's studies classes, where the vast majority of students were white, the working assumption was that feminism was racist. Students pejoratively referred to feminism as a "white middle-class women's movement." They accepted the accusations of many African American scholars that responsibility for that rested on the women in the movement, not also on those who failed to join.

In class, I offered a different explanation for the absence of large numbers of women of color in the women's movement. I agreed that it was unfortunate that feminists repeatedly failed in their efforts to recruit more than a handful of nonwhite women. But this failure was not, by itself, evidence of racism in the movement. Indeed, many white activists and early feminists were deeply troubled when their explicit attempts to build a broadly cross-racial and ethnically diverse women's movement bore little fruit. I explained that the racial divisions the students were experiencing at Colgate were not specific to the college or to the women's movement, but were the legacy of a shameful history of slavery and discrimination that poisoned relations everywhere in the society.

I could see that my students were unmoved. The charge of racism had become part of the conventional wisdom concerning the women's movement. One day in my introductory class, I decided to try a different approach. Rather than directly addressing feminism's alleged racism, I turned the discussion of strategies for social change to a debate about ethnic separatism within the women's movement. I assigned one group of students the task of arguing in favor of separate feminist organizations of Latina, African American, Asian American, and Native American women. Another group was asked to defend the position that such separatism set back the struggle for women's equality.

Wendy made the case for identity politics:

> Since diverse groups of women all have such different interests, they need to have separate organizations. Why should Latinas be forced to be in an organization with Asian American women

when each group has a totally different perspective? This way they can work on their own and not have to deal with the problem of trying to communicate with people who can't understand their point of view.

On the other side, students emphasized the negative impact of fragmentation. Susan pointed out that if these groups did not work together, their efforts might wind up in conflict with each other. Declaring that all women have so much in common, she asked, "What kind of an effect can a bunch of small groups have against sexism, compared to so many different women united around what they share? It's not even close! Working together is the only way we'll ever make any difference."

Despite this argument, when the students offered their own opinions at the end of the debate, the politics of racial identity prevailed. No one, including Susan, who had herself argued the integrationist case, believed that women should give up their separate organizations. Instead, several students spoke approvingly of the psychological importance of having a group where, as Genevieve put it, "others understand you." What students thought was inevitable was the centrality of race and ethnicity as the basis of political organizing. Arguments about common interests in child care, divorce legislation, economic equity, or health simply paled in light of the students' conviction that women from diverse identity groups thought, acted, and incontestably were just different.

Even when I pointed out that this position underlay the racial divisions on campus they themselves found so upsetting and frustrating, my students would not budge. They were unable to deal with the contradiction between their acceptance of identity politics and their desire for interracial harmony. Though they regretted it, the white students had come to accept the view that feminism/women's studies was a white woman's thing.

My efforts to reduce the balkanization on campus were largely unsuccessful. The guilt of the white students and the anger of the black students were simply too strong. Most white students lived in fear of offending women of color or of being accused of racial insensitivity.

Most black women refused to entertain the possibility that they could effectively address the sexism that troubled them by a united front with white feminists. Students on both sides of the divide felt saddened at the state of race relations on campus. But, nearly unanimously, they saw no way to break with the divisiveness demanded by identity politics.

CHAPTER 6

The Faculty

At most universities, women's studies' status as an academic program rather than a department differentiates it organizationally from other fields. Unlike traditional departments, women's studies is not able to hire its own faculty. Instead it "borrows" instructors from other academic departments to teach its courses.[1] At Colgate in 1996, for example, there were thirty-six faculty from a total of thirteen different departments participating in the program. Most women's studies courses were cross-listed in both the faculty member's home department and also as part of the women's studies curriculum. Faculty thus remained within their own departments when they offered women's studies courses. A handful of classes, including the introductory courses and capstone senior seminar, were taught by faculty released from their home departments.

This organizational structure created special problems, one of the most troublesome of which concerned new course approval. In the procedure that had been established before I arrived at Colgate, the Women's Studies Advisory Committee, consisting of all faculty members who taught in the program, voted on new courses. Course proposals were examined to determine whether they met the committee's two criteria for cross-listing. To be accepted, a course had to utilize gender as a central analytic category, and more than half of the reading material in the course had to be both by and about women.

---

1. The one exception at Colgate is the position of director, which is jointly appointed in the women's studies program and in the discipline-based department where the director's tenure resides.

I thought the first criterion unexceptional. All academic disciplines have the responsibility to delimit and make explicit their field of study. So it was with women's studies in specifying that an analysis of gender was its subject. However, to both parts of the second criterion—the standard that 50 percent of the reading material be both *by* and *about* women—I had strong objections.

First, I opposed using an author's sex as a litmus test for inclusion. I said as much at an early Women's Studies Advisory Committee meeting. I argued that it was impossible to evaluate either the quality or the content of written work simply by knowing whether the author is a woman or a man. This part of the second criterion I wanted to eliminate altogether. In opposition to my position, however, several faculty members argued that the sex of the author inevitably has an important influence on the content of written work. "Our women's studies students need to be immersed in women's perspectives," asserted Professor Frazier. "Right now the entire university should really be called 'Men's Studies' because all of academia takes a male perspective. Women's studies should be different. Only a woman researcher or writer can capture women's experience." In reply, I endorsed the recognition of women's scholarship as part of the mission of women's studies. But I denied that women have a unitary female perspective, and that it can be distinguished fundamentally from that of men. To ignore male writers because it is assumed that they cannot have a "woman's perspective," I argued, could deprive our students of important insights.

Professor Shepard took up the argument. She justified using sex as a criterion for assessing course material by recalling the history of discrimination against women in the academy. She noted that prejudice against women often had kept their intellectual work from being treated seriously and from being included in courses. It was because of this history, she concluded, that women's studies should mandate the use of women's writing in its courses.

Again I disagreed. Requiring the use of women authors would do nothing to alter the historical fact of discrimination. But, I pointed out, to exclude material on the basis of sex replicates historical censorship, this time with men instead of women as its target. I urged that as women's studies faculty, we adhere to our primary purpose—

educating our students by using the best materials available, regardless
of the sex of the author.

Before we had resolved this first issue, conversation turned to the
second part of the requirement, that more than half the content of
course readings must be about women. Most faculty seemed to think
that there could be no objection to this criterion for a women's studies course. Professor Wilcox looked right at me and said with some
sarcasm, "Well, I'm sure that at least no one objects to the idea of
studying *women* in a women's studies course." But I did object, and I
made my feelings known. My position was that, as a field, women's
studies had to study men as well as women. It was not possible to
fully explore the subjects important to women's studies without considering the relationship between women and men. Neither violence,
sexuality, socialization, nor family life, for example, could be studied
adequately on a single-sex basis. To require that an arbitrary percentage
of a course be solely about women denied faculty the flexibility to
teach about gender as they saw fit and as the specific subject matter
demanded.

This really offended a number of faculty. A history professor turned
on me, accusing me of advocating for men. "They don't need your
help," said Professor Tang angrily. "Everyone studies them all the
time, but what about women?" Professor Shepard rejoined the fray,
maintaining that as women we spend entirely too much of our time
analyzing our relationships to men. She argued that attention to
men was distracting from the real business of women's studies—to
understand women. To require that half the course content be about
women, in her opinion, was *minimal.* Other faculty then suggested
that, far from eliminating this requirement, we should make it even
more extensive. They proposed that every women's studies course
also be required to include writings by and about "minority women,
lesbians, and other oppressed groups."

Ultimately I could not convince the advisory committee of my point
of view. But neither did those who wanted to retain or expand the
restrictive criteria convince me. In the end, we compromised. I felt I
had to do so rather than hold out for the positions I believed in. As
the director for only a few months, I was still feeling my way. To be
unwilling to compromise on this issue would have contributed to an

environment of hostility that might have jeopardized the program and the other changes I was trying to make.

The compromise that emerged was more than a little strange. In typical academic style, the solution to the problem was at least as confusing as the problem itself. It involved changing an *and* to an *or*. The second criterion thereafter read: "More than half the reading material in a women's studies course will be by *or* about women." A careful parsing of this sentence reveals that the new guidelines in fact meant that the author's sex could be avoided as a determinant of merit, so long as more than half the readings were about women. At least that is how we agreed to interpret it. Though it did not fully satisfy me, at least with the change it was possible to ignore the author's sex as a criterion. And if in the future I found that good women's studies courses were being rejected by the committee because their content was less than half about women, I could always raise the issue again.

As it turned out, I was never required to revisit the issue of new course criteria. In practice, the advisory committee ignored its own guidelines in assessing new courses. When it came to actually approving new courses, faculty evidenced little concern about the criteria and only briefly discussed the content of proposed courses. Even when, a year later, I had convinced an anthropology professor to submit for approval a course on masculinity whose syllabus clearly violated the second criterion, it was accepted without objection. Indeed, in my experience, no course proposed for inclusion in the women's studies curriculum was ever rejected by the advisory committee. It was as if the symbolic discussion of the selection criteria and the rhetoric associated with it were more important to faculty members than the actual content of the courses that made up the curriculum.

There are feminist academics who believe that the "program" status of women's studies has outlived its usefulness. They argue passionately that women's studies instead deserves the same departmental status accorded other fields in the university. Those with this view believe that departmental autonomy is an essential stage in the development of feminist scholarship.

This question of departmental or program status was hotly debated at the 1996 National Women's Studies Association (NWSA) annual conference. At the preconference for administrators, I listened as several chairs of women's studies departments advanced the position that programs no longer had an effective role to play. A professor from a major midwestern university was particularly blunt: "Women's studies programs are seen as summer camp by the rest of the academy. Departments are where the serious teaching and research happen. Unless we become departments, we are just a joke." Another advocate of autonomy asserted: "Only in our own women's studies departments can we think our own thoughts and ask our own questions. As long as we are part of other disciplines, our free thought as feminists and the interdisciplinarity of feminist scholarship will inevitably be compromised and constrained." The internal politics of university life were also cited as supporting their claim for independence. "Now we count," declared the chair of a newly created department of women's studies. "We aren't outsiders any more. We have grown up."[2]

This strong advocacy evoked equally forceful responses from those opposed to departmental status. Some feared that a departmental structure would destroy women's studies' uniqueness, the essence of which, they believed, inhered in its status as programs. "We'll become just like every other academic discipline," one faculty member warned. "Don't you see? We'll be overprofessionalized petty bureaucrats, just like other academics." To her, it was only program status that enabled women's studies to emphasize the creation of community and cooperation over the hierarchy and competition that, as she put it, "infect the rest of the university." Those who took this position believed that program status alone could preserve what was best about women's studies.

Other faculty, particularly those who thought women's studies' aim should be the integration of gender into the entire university curriculum, also objected to departmental status. Their argument was that women's studies programs had already begun to transform traditional disciplines. A feminist perspective had begun to fundamentally change the way knowledge was developed and taught in the academy. Their fear was that a shift to departmental status would put an end to

2. See Judith A. Allen, "Strengthening Women's Studies in Hard Times: Feminism and Challenges of Institutional Adaptation" (*Women's Studies Quarterly* 25, nos. 1 and 2 [spring/summer 1997]: 358–87).

that process. The energy and effort required to create and maintain a department would leave little time for the transformation project. As a supporter of program status put it: "The real exercise of feminist power lies not in creating separate departments, but in pursuing integration of feminist ideas into teaching and research, in fundamentally changing everything."

It was disconcerting for me to listen to this debate. I agreed with no one! Though they differed among themselves, underlying all the arguments was a similar and I believed fundamental misconception: each speaker in her own way claimed that the study of women was somehow unique, fundamentally different from what went on in traditional disciplines. My twenty-five years as a feminist academic made me extremely skeptical of that claim. I believed on the contrary that women's studies was different only in its attention to a previously ignored subject matter—women and gender. With that important exception, the teaching and research done in women's studies was not inherently different from what goes on in other academic fields.

At Colgate, like those in other fields, women's studies classes vary tremendously, ranging from small seminars to large lecture courses, involving hands-on projects as well as traditional library research papers. In all these contexts, the instruction within the program is often very good indeed. But gifted teaching is not unique to women's studies. Just as elsewhere in the university, mediocre and even sometimes downright bad teaching is also present. There is nothing inherent in women's studies that inevitably creates exceptional teaching.

It is the same with research; unlike some of my colleagues, I do not believe that feminist research involves a distinctly female way of examining the world. To be sensitive to one's subjects and to try to see the world from their point of view are aspects of research that many women's studies scholars claim are unique to their field. But in fact these are rules that have long been accepted by all good social researchers, whether or not they are feminists.

To me, then, the answer to the question of the appropriate organizational form of women's studies was a pragmatic one: how best to ensure that scholars incorporate the previously neglected subjects of women and gender into their research and teaching. The specific structure needed to accomplish this will vary by institutional setting, but at Colgate the program approach has worked very well. It has encouraged and coordinated teaching and research on these subjects throughout the university, and provided opportunities for interaction among scholars interested in studying women and gender. At Colgate, women's studies does not require departmental status. Both it and its subject matter are viewed with the seriousness and respect they deserve.

In another discussion at the 1996 NWSA meeting, this time about the future of women's studies, a number of faculty warned that college administrators were attempting to dismantle their programs by replacing women's studies with "gender studies." According to these professors, the justification that administrators offered for the change was that both kinds of programs studied essentially the same subject matter, but that gender studies provided greater fairness and balance. Gender studies, they claimed, was more inclusive, and thus avoided the impression of discriminating against men.

Many women's studies faculty at the meeting angrily rejected the administrators' claim. They suggested instead that what was really motivating the drive for gender studies was a pervasive hostility to women's studies. One women's studies director explained: "Administrators on my campus who have always been opposed to women's studies are suddenly supersupportive of gender studies. It's clear that their goal is to do whatever they can to undermine our program." While a few spoke positively of the possibility of compromise by merging the two programs, most participants in the discussion believed that gender studies and women's studies were in a zero-sum struggle for survival. "Gender studies is nothing more than a way for antifeminists to get their foot in the door," asserted Professor Tappero, who reported being under pressure to replace her women's studies program with one in gender studies. "It means men can come into these programs and talk about men. The whole university curriculum will revert to being about men—men's history, men's literature, men's psychology. Before we know it, gender studies will hardly even include the study of women. Women's studies will disappear."

But the fact was that the increasing interest in gender studies had more complicated roots. Far from trying to destroy feminist scholarship on campus, some advocates of gender studies argued that it had distinct advantages for feminist teaching and research. A faculty member from a California state university explained why she had been in favor of her women's studies program's becoming a gender and women's studies program. Professor Donnelly reported that many different segments of the campus population, including some strong feminist students and faculty members, had lobbied for the change. She described for example the women's studies majors who thought that a new program name would eliminate the "feminist stigma" associated with women's studies. "Most of these students really wanted to study women," Professor Donnelly recalled, "but they were convinced they would never get jobs if they majored in women's studies." Others, according to Professor Donnelly, were trying to avoid the lesbian label that was attached at her campus to women's studies. Most feminist students, although conflicted about advocating a new program, nonetheless admitted that they were tired of fighting against stereotypes and of being treated "weird" because of their women's studies major.

Ironically, while some of Professor Donnelly's students supported gender studies because they thought it would protect them from a lesbian label, much of the gay, lesbian, and bisexual population on campus also favored the change. This group thought that, unlike women's studies, gender studies would make the exploration of sexuality its centerpiece. Gay students and faculty had long been critical of what they claimed was the neglect of "queer" issues by women's studies. Professor Donnelly also reported that faculty drawn to postmodern theory preferred *gender studies*. Uncomfortable with the theoretical construct of "women," they felt that gender studies would be less rooted in suspect sociological categories. The pressure from all these groups as well as from the administration proved too great, and the faculty in Professor Donnelly's women's studies program voted to change its name to Gender and Women's Studies. Professor Donnelly reassured her NWSA audience, however, that once the change had actually occurred, she had been forced to make only cosmetic changes in the program she administered. Nothing of importance to women's studies had been lost, and in fact the program had grown dramatically.

Professor Donnelly was simply not believed by the NWSA audience. The consensus was that the changes had to have been more than cosmetic. By far the concern that evoked the most emotional response in this regard was women's studies' special relationship to political activism. "Women's studies is an arm of the women's movement," declared one NWSA member. "With gender studies, or even gender and women's studies, the feminist activism inherent in women's studies will eventually be destroyed." Other faculty joined in assent.

In the discussion that ensued, I was struck by the unquestioned assumption that women's studies programs were and should be politically radical. One participant was explicit about her meaning: "Let's face it, preserving women's studies means preserving its lesbian separatist core." This emphasis on lesbian separatism drew dissent from some in the room. But no one questioned that women's studies should be tied to the women's movement. On this, there was consensus.

I finally spoke up in order to make several points. First, I said I believed too much emphasis was being placed on the name *women's studies*. As far as I could see, it did not much matter what the name of a particular program was; what mattered was its content. It was naive to think that a particular name would dictate what went on in a program. Conversely, a change of name would not necessarily alter a program's content.

But second, if the name change was trivial, I argued that the notion that women's studies programs should have a political agenda was not. In fact, it was alarming. If that was what was understood by *women's studies*, I wanted to register my strong dissent. Neither women's studies nor gender studies, I maintained, should be different from other academic subjects in this regard. Our goal as faculty should be to generate thought and knowledge, not a political agenda.

I went on to clarify one further point. My injunction against the narrow politicization of women's studies should not be confused with the deeply political content of its subject matter. In saying that women's studies should not be political, I was decidedly not arguing that it should avoid subjects that involve power relations. I took my own research as an example. Its content, I explained, has always been deeply political because I explore how social movements alter societies and the circumstances that give rise to those movements. Furthermore, it is in that sense of the word *political* that the emergence of women's studies itself can best be explained. Historically it took a political as well as an intellectual struggle to overcome the suppression of knowledge concerning women. Success in that fight was due in large measure to the prior emergence of the second wave of the women's movement in the late 1960s. Women's studies, then, is the result of politics, a change in power relations brought about by the women's movement, and it is about politics. But that is very different, I concluded, from the assertion that the field should be a political movement itself, dedicated to feminist activism.

I returned to Colgate from the conference deeply aware of the minority position I occupied within women's studies. For me, women's studies as a field can and should educate students about explicitly political subject matter without itself becoming politicized. When I teach about the women's movement, my classes explore its tactics, strategies, and impact while also examining opposing points of view on these subjects. In this context, I also offer my students my own judgments and the arguments on which I base them. I believe it would be irresponsible for me to feign neutrality concerning political issues that I have studied and about which I feel so deeply. I want my students to form their own opinions and have strong feelings about important subjects. Informing them of mine is a way of encouraging that process. In this, however, I am careful to also make credible the views of those who disagree with me, and to tell the students that they need to choose for themselves.

Intellectual engagement with political issues like feminism inevitably raises the question of activism. The latter logically follows from the former. But the classroom is not the appropriate place for activism or a political agenda. On the other hand, there is every reason for women's studies as a program to give students the chance to experience and learn from political activism. At Colgate, one of the roles of the center was to offer such opportunities. Center projects provided a way for students to express their own activism, whatever its specific content. But taking part in activist projects sponsored by the center was never required by women's studies courses. And the center never dictated the specific political positions that students should adopt.

In the fall of 1994, I was intrigued to read about the first conference of a new organization, the Women's Freedom Network (WFN). Led by prominent academic scholars, WFN described itself as committed to equality and to women's full participation in all aspects of society. WFN declared its support for the ERA and for women's reproductive rights. But it also criticized and positioned itself as an alternative to the "leading groups for and about women [that] represent extremist views not shared by the majority of American women." I was interested in this attempt to speak for the majority of American women in what WFN promised would be a new voice.

WFN conveyed the impression that it was distancing itself from both the right and the left concerning women's issues. It condemned organizations that rejected women's equality with men, lambasting both Phyllis Schlafly's Eagle Forum and Beverly LaHaye's Concerned Women for America. WFN said that it objected to the attempt by these organizations to convince women that "their own intellectual curiosity, professional talents, or other self interests should be subordinated to those of serving their families."[3] But even as it was attacking conservative opponents of feminism, WFN was also impatient with mainstream feminist organizations. According to WFN, national feminist groups like NOW were at fault for too often portraying women as victims and for denigrating women who "choose to be full-time mothers and homemakers." It was WFN's seeming iconoclasm, its apparent willingness to stand alone, that piqued my curiosity.

Though interested, I was also wary. I was put off that WFN routinely called feminist organizations extremist and had made reference to "The National Organization for Women and their radical feminist fellow travelers. . . ." This characterization seemed to me more smear than serious critique. I also was concerned that the organization was heavily funded by the conservative Ohlin Foundation. Despite WFN's attack on right-wing organizations like Schlafly's, I wondered how serious WFN was about its professed feminist commitment to equality. Perhaps their "feminism" was simply a ruse—a way to dupe women supportive of equality and critical of some aspects of feminism into endorsing a broader conservative agenda. I feared that in the end WFN's real goal might be simply to destroy existing feminist organizations.

3. Rita J. Simon, ed., *Neither Victim nor Enemy: Women's Freedom Network Looks at Gender in America* (Lanham, Md.: University Press of America, 1995), viii.

Despite these qualms, I could not deny that there were parts of WFN's critique of feminism with which I agreed. I, too, was concerned that feminists had failed to mobilize anything like a majority of American women. I thought WFN was right when it charged that some feminist claims about victimization were insufficiently supported by reliable data. I was encouraged that well-known feminists whom I respected—Nadine Strossen, Wendy Kaminer, and Dierdre English— were prominently featured as speakers at the upcoming Washington conference. I finally made up my mind to attend when I read that the conference ground rules would be tolerance and openness to diverse points of view.

The majority of the more than one hundred people attending the WFN conference were academics, including a number of women's studies faculty. Journalists and nonacademic policy analysts from national organizations and institutes made up the rest of the gathering. Most participants were not themselves active members of WFN. Rather, like me, they seemed to have come largely out of curiosity.

By the end of the second day of lectures and workshops, I was no longer uncertain about WFN. I knew that despite areas of overlap in our beliefs, we had too many fundamental disagreements for me to be a part of this group. I especially parted company with WFN's blanket hostility to government programs on behalf of women. When WFN members argued that no social policies were necessary to achieve gender equity because equality of opportunity had already been achieved between the sexes, I knew that this organization was not for me. Speaker after speaker at the conference savaged government interventions, including those whose obvious effect was to provide women with the opportunity to compete on fair terms. To my ears, this antigovernment stance closely resembled the right's "laissez-faire" anthem.

WFN's position seemed to be that women were already equal and independent. Organizational spokespeople minimized the existence of differences in the status of women and men in today's society. On that basis, they claimed there was no need for activist government policies to redress inequities.[4] Though speakers like Kaminer and Strossen pointed out the continued economic and social disadvan-

---

4. *Women's Freedom Network Newsletter* 1, no. 4 (1996): iv.

tages of women in American society, they had little impact on the tone of the conference.

My impression of a rightist agenda at the conference was further confirmed as I listened to speakers denounce existing feminist organizations. Rather than critiquing specific positions with which they disagreed, one presentation after another engaged in wholesale trashing of the feminist movement, of women's studies, and of what were constantly referred to as the excesses of radical feminists. My attempts to respond by describing the inclusive women's studies program I was creating at Colgate were lost, overwhelmed by the wholesale condemnation of the field. Indeed, the criticism of feminism at the conference was so persistent and angry that it often seemed as if WFN considered feminist organizations and feminism itself a greater danger than sexism.

I left the conference disappointed. I had hoped to find an organization brave enough to offer a critique of aspects of contemporary feminism, but also wise enough to acknowledge the need to continue the fight against sexism. Rather than being iconoclastic and independent as I had hoped, WFN members repeated tired clichés about government noninterference and feminist radicalism. I agreed with WFN's emphasis on women's right to choice in their lives. But WFN stopped right there—with a notion of rugged individualism. The feminist insight I accepted—that society can and should help to redress the disadvantages that women experience because of their sex—WFN denied. Because of that denial and despite its claim to the contrary, WFN as an organization, in my view, could not speak for the majority of women.

Critiques of women's studies have been many, but those that most interest me are those by women who consider themselves feminists. They offer their criticisms and suggestions for change in the hopes that they will strengthen feminism. But my experience is that my colleagues in women's studies programs rarely are willing to talk about what these critics have to say. Their criticisms are ignored or simply dismissed.

At a national women's studies administrators conference in Tempe, Arizona, in 1996, and later at a gathering of California women's studies faculty, I presented and critiqued the ideas of several of these feminist critics.[5] Reaction to my presentation at the two meetings could hardly have been more different. At the first, I received a polite response, though many participants were reluctant to fully engage the issues raised by the critics. At the second, no such decorum existed. I was denounced for consorting with the enemy.

My remarks at both meetings concentrated on three major complaints raised by critics. First, feminism and women's studies focus too much on and exaggerate women's victimization; second, they are dominated by psychological, identity, and cultural issues to the neglect of the economic and practical problems that are uppermost for most women; and third, separatism and inadequate intellectual rigor characterize women's studies programs.

The first issue was victimization. While acknowledging that women have been and often still are oppressed by sexism, the critics' argument is that feminism has been guilty of glamorizing that oppression, turning victimization into a positive source of identity. Doing so, they say, not only reinforces traditional stereotypes of women as passive and powerless, but also trivializes the significant gains achieved by feminist activism. Many critics worry that a preoccupation with victimization has the politically debilitating effect of convincing women that it is hopeless to try to take control of their own lives.[6]

After summarizing their critique, I turned to a discussion of the extent to which my experience at Colgate had corroborated this point of view. I argued that women's studies students did tend to be preoccupied with the ways in which women have been oppressed. In the first flush of recognizing the real harm done to women by sexist institutions and attitudes, undergraduates are often so outraged that they have difficulty focusing on anything but the horror of first discovery. For many students, even with the passage of time, victimization remains

5. A version of these comments appeared in Joan D. Mandle, "Sisterly Critics" (*NWSA Journal* 11, no. 1 [spring 1999]: 97–109). See also Joan D. Mandle, "A Response to 'There Are No Victims in This Class' " (*NWSA Journal* 11, no. 1 [spring 1999]: 114–16).

6. See especially Rene Denfeld, *The New Victorians: A Young Woman's Challenge to the Old Feminist Order* (New York: Warner, 1995); Naomi Wolf, *Fire with Fire: The New Female Power and How It Will Change the Twenty-first Century* (New York: Random House, 1993).

the defining characteristic of their feminism, often causing them to be politically paralyzed.

I suggested that women's studies faculty could counter this over-reaction by helping students put women's oppression in a wider in-tellectual context. This could be done by exploring the gains women have made toward greater equality. Attention to past improvements in women's status would help to put students in touch with the possi-bilities of even further progress. Instead of offering only a bleak litany of the profound problems women have had and continue to face, I suggested that women's studies should provide more of a balance.

The second theme common to the critics was that women's stud-ies neglects important issues of social policy. The claim is that the dominant concerns of women's studies are with individual identity, postmodern theory, and cultural and literary analysis. A serious grap-pling with the social structure, institutions, and policies that support sexism is not a high priority. But the latter, say the critics, is what is required for a real understanding of both how to eliminate women's continued disadvantages and how to construct a society of equality.

In my experience, I explained, most women's studies students were more interested in issues of their own personal identity and lifestyle than in social analysis. Many seek in women's studies and feminism the guidance to resolve their own life struggles. But I argued that women's studies could and should resist becoming therapeutically or individually oriented in response to student pressure. Instead, we could help our students see beyond a feminism of identity that con-fines itself to psychological self-examination. Higher education does have a role to play in young people's search to discover who they are. But women's studies can best facilitate that search by revealing the connections between students' interests, which are so often personal and self-absorbed, and the needs, cares, and problems of others in their society.[7]

The final accusation I took up was the critics' complaint that wo-men's studies programs see themselves as a safe space for women,

---

7. See Elizabeth Fox-Genovese, *"Feminism Is Not the Story of My Life": How Today's Feminist Elite Has Lost Touch with the Real Concerns of Women* (New York: Doubleday, 1996); and Denfeld, *New Victorians*.

separate from and in opposition to the academy as a whole. Critics charge that this isolation is constructed by excluding male faculty and students as well as women who do not self-identify as feminists. In this, the intellectual rigor of women's studies programs is also often questioned.[8]

Again I reported that my experiences at Colgate suggested the need to take this critique seriously. I discussed the numerous occasions on which faculty had actively opposed including in women's studies men or even women whose views did not conform to feminist orthodoxy. Furthermore, in my experience, there had been women's studies professors who definitely found virtue in an absence of rigor. To be sure, instructors of this kind did not characterize the entire program; neither were they limited only to women's studies courses. My argument, however, was that women's studies administrators needed to be aware of such tendencies and be vigilant about shaping programs that maintained high levels of intellectual sophistication.

I concluded my talk by encouraging the program administrators to engage in a critical assessment of their own efforts. I acknowledged that it was difficult for those of us committed to women's studies to be open to the suggestions of critics. But, I warned, just because feminism and women's studies have often been falsely indicted does not mean that we should view all criticisms simply as attacks that seek to destroy what we have built. Instead we need to take a hard look at that edifice and have the courage to change what needs changing.

At my first presentation of these arguments, though disagreement was expressed, many in the audience were willing to be self-critical. Professor Jarrell, a women's studies administrator from Maine, described her difficulties with several of her faculty members who "sat around with their students in class and, rather than teaching, simply talked about their feelings." She asked for suggestions about how she could encourage a more demanding classroom environment without violating the academic freedom of those faculty. The room came alive with ideas, ranging from her forcefully expressing concern to the faculty involved, to organizing teaching seminars for them.

---

8. Daphne Patai and Noretta Koertge, *Professing Feminism: Cautionary Tales from the Strange World of Women's Studies* (New York: Basic Books, 1994).

Later in the discussion, a faculty member from a small liberal arts college in Maryland vigorously defended the creation of a safe space for women, maintaining that it was a legitimate concern for women's studies programs. Though I was braced for others to agree, I was pleasantly surprised when her comments evoked little support. Instead, the discussion turned to an exchange of views about how to attract more faculty and students to women's studies. Several directors offered specific accounts of how they had successfully reached out to others on their campus. At the end of the session in Tempe, I was more than satisfied that a fruitful exchange of ideas had occurred.

A year and a half later, when I presented the same material as a keynote address at the women's studies conference in California, the response of my audience was much more hostile. The organizers of this second conference had attended the conference in Tempe and heard me speak there. In inviting me to California, they explained, "we want people to hear your ideas, even though we know that they are pretty controversial." After the positive experience I had at the Tempe conference, I was completely unprepared for what I faced in California. For almost forty minutes after my presentation, the content of my speech was attacked by members of the audience. Speakers questioned both my motivation and the prudence of discussing the topic I had selected. I was even criticized for what I did not say. One person rhetorically asked, "Why are you neglecting the important problems of African American women by concentrating on what these privileged white women are saying, none of which is true anyway?"

My attempts to respond were to no avail. But what was most distressing was that no one was even willing to entertain the possibility that the critics might have something useful to say. They simply denied that women's studies programs remotely resembled what the critics described. They stonewalled, refusing to acknowledge the possible existence of problems. "I don't recognize a single word you've said, in either my own women's studies program or in any other one I know about," said one speaker, capturing the essence of at least a half dozen other objections. "Colgate must be unique, having all the problems you see there. But you have no right to assume that other programs are like yours."

At first I badly misinterpreted what was going on. After the first few directors reported that their programs were virtually problem-free, I congratulated them. I had not yet gotten the point. The reality of what I was dealing with became clearer, however, when I asked them to share how it was that they had been so successful in avoiding the difficulties that the critics had outlined. This was a complete nonstarter, because for these faculty there was no need for a discussion of strategies to avoid problems. There simply were none. "All these problems are just myths created by the critics," someone in the audience declared; "it's a kind of disinformation to delegitimate women's studies programs."

As my exasperation grew, I suggested that since it was highly unlikely that every one of the programs represented here was perfect, all this denial of problems smacked of avoidance, confirming the critics' belief that women's studies faculty were unwilling to be self-critical. In response, someone who I knew generally agreed with me stood up to denounce my presentation. "Don't you know that Fox-Genovese has publicly spoken out against abortion rights for women? Why should we believe anything she has to say?" asked Professor Grinham. This was awful. Professor Grinham was implying that because of Fox-Genovese's position on abortion, her comments on women's studies should be discredited. I was shocked to hear Professor Grinham dismissing someone on the basis of an ideological litmus test. I, too, disagreed with Fox-Genovese on abortion as well as on a number of other issues. But those disagreements did not change my intellectual responsibility to consider her views. I said as much in reply to Professor Grinham. But I was aware that by that time nothing I said was being heard. Having decided that I was an enemy of feminism, my audience had erected a wall between us and either ignored or discounted everything I had to say.

Only after the luncheon ended, and in private, did anyone admit to agreeing with my point of view. As others left the room to attend afternoon workshops, three women approached me. Clearly upset at how I had been treated, each apologized for failing to defend me publicly. They were afraid to speak up, they said. "It was kind of intimidating," offered one, as the others nodded in agreement. Her admission confirmed yet another of the objections raised by the critics. Women's studies still was having trouble encouraging a free and open dialogue.

The experience of this conference shook me. I was hurt by the attack. But I was also saddened at the defensiveness of my colleagues. Their posture could only lead to trouble. Without openness to outside criticism, women's studies would suffer from insularity. Furthermore, because women's studies' participants and supporters were frequently too intimidated to air disagreements, the recognition of problems, as well as possible solutions, would be unlikely to emerge from within the field.

After the conference ended, I drove home with the conference organizer who had invited me to speak. She was very apologetic for having "gotten you into this mess," as she put it, but rather than seeing the attack on me as a problem deep within women's studies, she sought an explanation elsewhere. "Maybe it was the size of the room. It was so much bigger than at Tempe, and you were so much farther away from people. Or maybe it was different because it was a keynote address." But she also faulted me: "I think maybe you had a different tone this time." She suggested that if I gave the talk again, I should begin with a longer introduction featuring positive comments about women's studies.

In the car with us for the long ride home was Professor Ambler, who at the luncheon had been one of those who most vigorously denied that I was describing problems that really existed in women's studies. To my astonishment, she proceeded, in the car, to contradict what she had publicly stated not two hours earlier at the luncheon. "I have to admit that your comments described to a T the women's studies program I taught in eight years ago. It had every one of the problems you mentioned and more. In fact, that's why I left. I don't teach women's studies anymore."

I was disgusted that Professor Ambler was willing to tell me privately of the problems in the women's studies program in which she had taught, but that she had somehow been unable to remember to mention those problems when she had denounced me. But the time to fight had passed. The ride home continued in silence after Professor Ambler rendered a final judgment on my talk, "I really think we don't need anyone else trashing women's studies. There are enough people who want to do that every day."

Ending

I directed Colgate's women's studies program for six years. Throughout, it was clear that a handful of faculty, all of whom had been closely associated with women's studies before my arrival, were unhappy with its new direction. Among this group, two showed their disapproval by refusing to have anything to do with women's studies other than teaching their classes. They never set foot in the center. Several others, who also voiced objections, nonetheless grudgingly continued to serve on the advisory committee and from time to time participated in center activities.

I regretted the alienation of these veterans of the old women's studies program. But their disaffection was not actually as harmful to the program as I feared it might be. Overall faculty involvement in women's studies grew every year, with new courses and activities widely supported, especially by younger faculty. The active engagement of increasing numbers of students in the center and the enthusiasm of new faculty more than offset the lack of support from dissatisfied members of the old guard. Nonetheless, my inability to convince those faculty to change their attitude toward the program continued to bother me. I was also troubled that they would not openly discuss with me the criticisms they so obviously harbored.

This changed three years into my tenure as director when one of that small group, Professor Braune, was promoted to a high-level, policy-making position in the college's administration. Soon after her appointment, she and I became embroiled in a conflict, which, though extremely unpleasant, served to clarify for me her objections to the program and the center. What I learned was that her notion of women's studies was almost identical to that of the previous director and thus fundamentally opposed to mine. Professor Braune believed that women's studies' main task ought to be constructing a "women's community" within the college, especially among the faculty.

The conflict between us emerged in a most unlikely way. During the spring of 1994, it was announced that the college was closing down the dormitory where the Center for Women's Studies was housed. I had to find a new location for the center by the following fall. After lobbying several administrators, I obtained the promise of an even larger and more desirable space. I immediately starting planning for the center's move. I envisioned an occasion for celebrating a new beginning that would include the entire college, gain even more exposure for the center, and draw in new people.

As I was considering the most effective way to do this, I realized that the center's move would coincide with the twentieth-fifth anniversary of coeducation at Colgate. A combined campus celebration of the reopening of the center and the anniversary of coeducation would be just the thing, I thought. It would reinforce the message that women's studies was the centerpiece of the college's coeducational mission, and that women's studies included everyone. Since the program did not have the funds to mount such a gala, I set out to seek the administration's support.

As I began to make inquiries I encountered a perplexing reluctance to endorse my idea. I was met with a combination of equivocation and delay. By August nothing specific had been done, and it was becoming clear to me that no joint celebration was likely. However, it was only later that I learned the real reason for the resistance to my plan. The opposition was directly related to the fact that a previous celebration of coeducation, held in 1990, had been, by almost everyone's account, an unmitigated disaster. Becky Albright, the staff member who had helped organize the event, told me what happened. Funded by the alumni office, the weekend of October 5 had been billed as "The First Twenty Years: A Celebration of Women at Colgate." It was conceived as the kickoff to a concerted effort to involve more alumnae in donating to the college. This marked an important change, since previous fundraising and alumni organizing had concentrated almost exclusively on male graduates. The administration had finally come to realize that women graduates were numerous enough to represent a significant potential source of financial support. The twentieth-year celebration, it was hoped, would bring alumnae back to the campus and signal a new commitment to recognizing women's history and place at Colgate.

The response from alumnae was greater than anticipated. Over one hundred women, many accompanied by their families, returned to Hamilton for the reunion. The weekend was organized as a series of panels and workshops, ranging from those that explored the current Colgate experience for undergraduate women—its curriculum, residential life, and women's studies program—to those that facilitated alumnae networking and discussions of how to balance work, family, and career. A Friday evening keynote was given by a well-known journalist and television personality who had graduated from Colgate with the first class of women. She talked about that first year and about how well Colgate had prepared her for her career. The weekend was off to a great start. "The whole thing seemed like such a huge success," recalled Becky with a sigh. "Until Sunday."

The crisis occurred at the final event, an alumnae "conversation" with the president of the college concerning the future of women at Colgate. President Jeffries, who had only recently come to Colgate, offered opening remarks about his personal as well as the college's commitment to higher education for women. According to Becky, the moment he finished speaking, the celebration suddenly was transformed into a nasty attack on everything about Colgate—all in the name of feminism. In what was an apparently well-orchestrated plan, one alum after another stepped up to the microphone to accuse President Jeffries and the college of failing to provide undergraduate women with a positive learning environment. They railed at the continued dominance of fraternities, complained that women at Colgate were not safe, and expressed outrage at the college's alleged unwillingness to take strong action when rapes were committed on campus. When President Jeffries tried to respond to the accusations, Becky said that he was shouted down. He was denounced personally for failing to provide what was referred to as real coeducation. "No one was listening to anyone else, anyhow. Everyone was just shouting. I was shaking like a leaf," Becky reported.

After hearing the story, I saw why members of the administration had reacted so negatively to my suggestion for a joint celebration of the twenty-fifth anniversary of coeducation and women's studies. But it still was not clear to me why that Sunday morning had turned out as it had. Professor Weiner, a faculty member in English and women's studies who had been there, explained it in more detail during a later conversation:

> It was only a small group of alums who decided to take over the meeting. They didn't have any real information about what was going on at Colgate. They were still angry about things that had happened to them fifteen or more years ago. The meeting got really emotional when they charged that women undergraduates were not safe. That alarmed everyone. And none of us who actually knew what was happening on campus could get a word in. Some who tried to say that their experience at Colgate was positive were denounced along with President Jeffries. Everyone was made to feel that if you had anything good to say about Colgate you were condoning sexual violence against women.

The president had obviously been traumatized that day, but I thought that, if provided with the opportunity, he might want to try to rectify the damage created by the debacle that had occurred five years earlier. I would offer him a second chance to celebrate and publicly affirm Colgate's commitment to women. I explained to President Jeffries my idea for a celebration focused not on alums but on educating the student body and faculty concerning the importance of coeducation. An all-college event endorsed by the president would make clear to everyone that the college believed in both coeducation and in women's studies.

He agreed. President Jeffries said he would support a campuswide celebration, focused on the reopening of the center. I was thrilled with the chance to showcase the new center in this way and immediately began organizing for the day of the celebration. The student assistants decorated the new center and prepared an exhibit depicting the history of women at Colgate as well as pamphlets outlining the history of women's studies. They also planned tours of the site for the day of the celebration to show it off to faculty and students.

Just as we were really making progress, Professor Braune, newly appointed to her administrative position, called me into her office. I had no idea what she wanted, but it never occurred to me that she might object to the celebration. I naively assumed that anyone who cared about women's studies, not to mention a strong feminist like herself, could not but welcome the college's attention to the center and the role of women at Colgate. How wrong I was. But at first I was confused, because Professor Braune avoided directly stating her opposition to the idea of a joint celebration. She began by talking about how much she and I shared. "We both are radicals and feminists within a patriarchal institution," she confided. Then, without a pause, she stated that she wanted to be sure I was including everyone in the celebration. Ignoring what she had to say about our presumed shared radicalism, I replied, "Of course. You know our policy is to include everyone in all women's studies events. That's why I am so excited about this celebration. It really looks like the whole college will come out." She seemed unimpressed, and again she urged me to make sure that no one was excluded, stating: "I think some people are feeling left out."

By this time, I was completely baffled. I simply could not figure out what she meant. Furthermore, her reference to Colgate as "patriarchal" was puzzling. By what definition could Colgate, with so many women, including herself, in powerful administrative positions, be described as patriarchal—especially on the eve of its launching a major celebration of women? As I puzzled on this, Professor Braune broadened her criticism beyond the celebration to the women's studies program itself. Both my plan for the celebration and my shaping of the program shared the same flaw, in her view. She believed that a closely knit community was the only way to meet the real needs of women at Colgate. What was needed was a safe space, "a place where women can go to be renewed and show their commitment to other women." In her opinion, neither the program nor the celebration sufficiently contributed to "doing something special to make sure that women are protected at Colgate." For Professor Braune, a celebration of coeducation "should create solidarity in the women's community at Colgate," not dilute it through an all-campus celebration.

Our differences were finally clear. Now I knew why Professor Braune and the handful of other original women's studies faculty had, despite my efforts to induce them to participate more fully, largely absented themselves from the program. By constructing an outward-looking program and concentrating on building a center that addressed the needs of students rather than servicing a small group of faculty, I had offended them and denied them the exclusive community they wanted. These were the "left out" people on whose behalf Professor Braune was criticizing the celebration.

But what shocked me most was yet to come. "You know," she said, her voice rising with emotion, "what we really need is a situation where the kinds of honest sentiments expressed at the Sunday breakfast meeting five years ago at the twentieth anniversary can be stated openly." I could hardly believe what I was hearing. Here was one of a handful of the most powerful administrators on campus applauding a gratuitous attack on the college and its president, based on charges that she had to know did not remotely correspond to the school's reality. What could she have been thinking?

I left Professor Braune's office dumbstruck. During my meeting with her, I had tried to defend both the celebration and the program. But there was no bridging the gap between her conception of a strong women's studies program and mine. Professor Braune's endorsement of what had gone on five years earlier reflected her deep conviction that women students and especially faculty needed a place into which to retreat for mutual support. I believed, on the contrary, that it would be wrong to use women's studies to try to construct a separatist enclave. Not only would it isolate feminists from the rest of the campus, but it would forfeit the opportunity to educate women and men, students and faculty, about feminist issues. It boggled my mind that Professor Braune was so hostile to what was clearly a successful program. What was worse, I knew that Professor Braune's hostility represented more than an academic disagreement over inclusivity. She had the power to destroy the celebration and perhaps even the program I had built.

I fought back by doing what I otherwise would have tried hard to avoid: that very afternoon, I went over Professor Braune's head and made an appointment to see President Jeffries. In order to ensure that the kind of celebration he had signed on to would actually occur, it was important for him to know that someone as high in his administration as Professor Braune opposed the plan. In the president's office, I repeated Professor Braune's conversation with me. She had herself supplied me with the ammunition I needed; President Jeffries could not but be furious at her approval of the attack on him five years earlier. When I had finished, President Jeffries did not say a word about Professor Braune. Instead he spoke as if he were issuing a policy directive: "I want you to know that you, your program, and this celebration have my full support and that of my entire administration."

I was of course relieved, but it was nevertheless with some anxiety two days later that I responded to an invitation from Professor Braune asking me to go to lunch. My concern, however, soon dissipated. For over an hour, she talked about how excited she was about the plans for a campuswide celebration of coeducation and the center. Not a negative word about exclusion or women's studies passed her lips.

The joint celebration of coeducation and the new center's grand opening was a great success. Posters, buttons, flyers, and balloons had been distributed all over campus, and at the hour of the celebration, the chapel bells—rarely rung at Colgate—marked its beginning. President Jeffries welcomed the gathering of several hundred outside the center, as Professor Braune joined another faculty member and two students in cutting the bright yellow inaugural ribbon strung across the front door. Twenty-five candles decorated a giant anniversary cake that was distributed to the even larger number of faculty and students who came to a reception that followed the ribbon-cutting ceremony. The turnout was gratifying and the festive mood on campus was exhilarating. Everyone was aware that Colgate was recognizing the women in its midst and renewing its commitment to equal education. For the moment, my views concerning inclusiveness had prevailed. But I knew that the conflict between Professor Braune and myself still festered.

It was not until over a year later that this disagreement resurfaced. During the fall semester of 1995, Professor Braune again called me into her office, this time for what I expected to be a pro forma discussion of the renewal of my five-year term as director of women's studies. Instead, she informed me of her intention to replace me. At first, the only explanation she would offer for my removal was that it was "time for someone else to direct women's studies at Colgate. It will be exciting for you to return to teaching sociology." Although I had not expected any of this, I told Professor Braune that I would not give up women's studies easily. I wanted to continue to direct the program.

In the lengthy discussion that followed, Professor Braune indicated that when she had polled the faculty about replacing me she had found strong support for both me and the program. "However," she continued, "there were several faculty who complained that the program is too oriented toward the students. They say they miss the solidarity with other faculty women." Her real objection to my tenure as director, however, came out when she charged that in drawing so many students and faculty into women's studies, "especially those new to feminism, I think you have neglected and excluded the voices of those most strongly committed to feminism."

This was familiar territory. It was clear that nothing had changed since our earlier conversation. Again, I tried fruitlessly to convince her that the primary mission of women's studies should be to promote education and scholarship, not to meet the personal needs of women students or faculty. I denied excluding anyone. Faculty who complained about being silenced, I charged, were simply those who disagreed with the direction I had taken women's studies. They of course had every right to refuse to participate in a program whose goals were inconsistent with their own preferences. But, I concluded, that should not be confused with being silenced or excluded.

Though Professor Braune offered me a number of inducements to vacate the directorship, including other administrative positions and a research stipend, I bluntly told her that I would not be bought off. I was not interested in more money or any other administrative position. I felt I had something unique to contribute in women's studies and I wanted to continue to build on the successful program. My goal was to ensure that even more Colgate students were included in the process of feminist education. We argued inconclusively. After an exhausting session that failed to come to closure, Professor Braune insisted on continuing our conversation the next day. And then the day after that. Ultimately, this went on for a total of eleven hours over four days. Neither of us would concede. It was during the last of these marathon sessions, however, that Professor Braune finally went too far. She accused me of resisting her decision to remove me only because she was, of all things, a woman. I was furious! "You know better than that," I flared. "Don't insult me by implying that I treat people differently depending on their gender. I don't." The meeting and our extended dialogue ended abruptly on that note. Professor Braune said she would call me with her decision. A week later, Professor Braune reappointed me as director for an additional three-year term. I was offered no explanation for this about-face. Though I had hoped for a five-year renewal, I accepted her offer and continued as before.

But in the end, Professor Braune won. One year into my new three-year term, personal circumstances forced me to take a leave of absence from Colgate. In my place, Professor Braune appointed two faculty members, Professors Kim and Rothburn, as acting codirectors of the program. Both these women had been close to the original director, and although they had participated in women's studies during my tenure, they had been among those critical of the direction in which I had taken the program.

That a change in tone was about to occur in the program was foreshadowed by a visit, by Professors Kim and Rothburn, even before they agreed to serve as acting directors, to the dean of students. According to Dean Hinckley, they notified him that when they took over women's studies, "the safety of women students at Colgate will be our highest priority." In this way they all but explicitly repudiated my policy of denying that women's studies should shoulder responsibility for the security of women on campus. Dean Hinckley was upset by his meeting with Professors Kim and Rothburn, especially when they questioned his commitment to preventing sexual assaults against undergraduates. He worried to me about the future of what had been a positive relationship between his office and women's studies.

During the year I was away, the emphasis of women's studies was redirected back to the emotional support of the faculty. In the annual report that Professors Kim and Rothburn submitted at the end of the year, they highlighted their success in providing "opportunities for women faculty to get together informally." As in the reports of the first director of the program, the goal of "building community" appeared prominently. Resumed also was the practice of excluding men from the beginning-of-the-year faculty reception. When the women's studies secretary questioned whether they really meant to exclude men, she was told that it would be too expensive to invite men to the reception. And in response to the intern's explicit objection to barring men from the event, Professor Rothburn stated: "Men wouldn't come anyway, so why invite them."

In short, with my departure, women's studies quickly reverted to much of what I had fought against: an emphasis on the psychological needs of women as sexual victims; the view that women faculty are a beleaguered group that needs its own supportive community from which men should be excluded; and rhetoric that differentiates the role of women's studies from that of other disciplines, by emphasizing the goals of protecting women and constructing community.

Halfway through my leave of absence, I realized that I would need an additional year away from Colgate. Immediately after I was granted a second leave, Professor Braune, without so much as informing me, permanently replaced me, appointing Professor Rothburn as director of Colgate's women's studies program.

When I reflect on my experience during the years I directed women's studies, what I remember most is the tapestry of people and incidents that I have built this memoir around. But in thinking of the lessons I learned and what I took away with me, I continually come back to two things. One is the absolute necessity for scholars and educators to incorporate an analysis of gender if we are to make sense of what goes on in our society. The second is the critical importance of women's studies' presence on college campuses today. These two are not really separable. Because gender analysis casts an essential light on important problems in society, it deserves the prominent place in the intellectual life of higher education that women's studies has secured for it.

Recognition of the importance of feminist thought in the academy is relatively recent. As I was growing up I was alternately confused, saddened, and furious that I was treated differently than boys. I could not understand why—simply because I was a girl—no one was willing to take me seriously when I spoke or objected to something, or suggested that things should be different. I did not fully escape this kind of dismissal even when, in the early 1960s, I enrolled as an undergraduate at Vassar, an all-women's college. The rejection of women as intellectual equals also tarnished what a few years later turned out to be the most formative experience of my life. Drawn by visions of equality and justice to join the Civil Rights and antiwar movements, I, along with other women, were shocked to find that even there we were not accorded equal respect.[1] Out of that experience, the women's liberation movement emerged. From it, in turn, came the feminist analysis that generated women's studies. I can remember the utter relief I felt when for the first time I encountered a serious academic attempt to understand women and their role in society.[2] Though I did not always agree with what was said, I finally had a context in which to seek insight both into what was happening to me and other women, and into the possibilities for change.

I understand my experience in women's studies at Colgate to be part of the process of my continuing that intellectual exploration. Recalling the absence of intellectual analysis of women in the university curriculum when I was an undergraduate makes me appreciate women's studies. It provided me with the opportunity to immerse myself in and share with my students the study of gender. Directing the program allowed me to pursue a vision of feminist intellectual engagement, one that went beyond the classroom. The center became an important locus on campus of student exploration of political and social issues. As such it was a special place that students valued and where they could feel comfortable. This occurred not because it was a "safe space," but because it was something more nearly its opposite. It was a location where students knew they would find serious intellectual discourse and diverse points of view, where their ideas about feminism would be tested.

I am sorry that in the end, my perspective on women's studies was not shared by the university. But its decision in this regard does not

---

1. Sara M. Evans, *Personal Politics: The Roots of Women's Liberation in the Civil Rights Movement and the New Left* (New York: Random House, 1980).

2. See also Rachel Blau DuPlessis and Ann Snitow, eds., *Feminist Memoir Project: Voices from Women's Liberation* (New York: Three Rivers Press, 1998).

diminish the importance of the task of creating an inclusive feminist dialogue. That objective can still stand as a goal for women's studies programs. As I tried to tailor my vision of feminist education to Colgate, I made some mistakes and offended some of my colleagues. My own personal style and Colgate's circumstances were of course unique—but the problems and issues that arose there are not. Women's studies programs everywhere must grapple with the same questions I struggled with at Colgate. Whether to include or exclude men; the problem of how to involve more women of color; and arguments about pornography, coeducation, psychological therapy, sexuality, and self-censorship are always present. Many of these same issues trouble the feminist movement outside the university as well. It is unfortunate that in neither context are these difficulties often enough addressed directly.

In academic programs within universities, I believe that what is critical is not how these issues are resolved, but that they are addressed openly, as part of an educational process. What the Colgate program demonstrates is that these and related subjects of community, identity politics, political activism, and social change are of great intellectual interest to students and faculty. If given the opportunity, they will flock to discussions of feminism that are presented in an open and tolerant fashion, where all points of view are welcomed. Students and faculty will be willing to think about gender in their own lives, and take or teach courses in women's studies, if they are not frightened away by feminist faculty and students more interested in establishing their own radical credentials than in exploring these subjects with others, including those who may disagree.

In my years as director I had both successes and failures, but the experience of creating a program to which students were drawn by the opportunity to talk about important issues was constantly exciting. It was gratifying to watch their usual "cool" fall away before the chance to think and talk about big issues that really mattered. Though it angered some, the constant theme at the center and in the program as a whole was that feminism and women's studies was about all of us, about justice, about fairness. With a consistent commitment to this goal, it was possible to create an environment of serious discourse and to resist the temptations of exclusive community and safe space. This strategy was seen by some as insufficiently feminist. But that was a risk I was willing to take. I did so in order to craft a program that communicated to everyone at Colgate that an uncensored exploration of gender can help us understand not only some of the ways that the world is unfair, but also some of the ways we might make it better.

About the Author

Director of Women's Studies at Colgate University in Hamilton, New York, for six years, Joan D. Mandle is currently Associate Professor of Sociology there. She is the author of *Women and Social Change in America*, among other books.